ORGANISATIONAL CHANGE THROUGH PARTNERSHIP

Promise, Performance and Prospects for Irish Firms

John O'Dowd

The Liffey Press

Published by
The Liffey Press
Ashbrook House, 10 Main Street
Raheny, Dublin 5, Ireland
www.theliffeypress.com

© 2010 John O'Dowd

A catalogue record of this book is
available from the British Library.

ISBN 978-1-905785-50-6

The author and publishers would like to thank the Irish
Labour Relations Commission, in particular its Chief Executive
Kieran Mulvey, for their support of this publication.

Printed in the Republic of Ireland by Gemini International

ORGANISATIONAL CHANGE
THROUGH PARTNERSHIP

About the Author

John O'Dowd is in independent consultant specialising in organisational change and dispute resolution. He has worked with a wide range of organisations helping employers and trade unions to design and develop effective change management processes and to resolve disputes arising from organisational changes. He is a former director of the National Centre for Partnership and former general secretary of the Civil Public and Services Union. In 1998 he published *Employee Partnership: A Guide for Managers*, Oak Tree Press, and in 2005 he co-authored with Jerome T. Barrett *Interest-Based Bargaining: A Users Guide*, Trafford Publishing. He was awarded his doctorate in 2006.

CONTENTS

LIST OF TABLES AND FIGURES

List of Tables

List of Figures

INTRODUCTION

In the late 1990s in Ireland there was a surge of interest among employers, trade unionists and policy makers in the idea that workplace relationships and organisational performance could be significantly enhanced through a 'partnership' approach to organisational change. A 'partnership' approach meant that managers, union representatives and employees would work together through joint bodies to effect changes and to resolve difficulties using a 'problem-solving' as opposed to a conflictual approach. This idea was not a new one on the international stage at that time. Most employers and trade unionists in Ireland, however, at the time engaged little together outside the collective bargaining arena. Indeed, the conventional portrayal of management-union relations at workplace level was that these were of a strong 'them and us' type with low trust, low levels of employee involvement in change, considerable employee fear of change, and frequent resistance to change. Thus, a 'partnership' approach to organisational change represented for many managers and trade unionists a vision – however attractive and desirable – that was far removed form current realities.

At the time, some industrial relations practitioners and policy makers in Ireland were familiar with headline cases of 'labour-management co-operation' from North America such as the Ford Saturn Plant through the industrial relations literature as well as through study visits to US sites arranged by, among others, the

Irish Productivity Centre (IPC). The IPC was a publicly funded training and consulting organisation that was jointly owned by the Irish Business and Employers' Confederation (IBEC) and the Irish Congress of Trade Unions (ICTU).

ICTU had been to the fore during the 1990s in encouraging trade unions to take a more positive and strategic approach towards workplace change provided that employers were willing to involve then sufficiently in the change process. This renewed interest in employee involvement culminated in the 1996 national programme, *Partnership 2000*, which provided for the first time a nationally agreed framework for the development of partnership at workplace or organisation levels in the private and public sectors. Around this time also, a number of companies and their trade unions agreed to develop voluntary partnership structures through which they would introduce new forms of work organisation aimed at enhancing productivity and competitiveness. For unions and employees, these partnerships offered the promise of increased influence in workplace decision-making as well as improvements in pay and conditions and the quality of working life generally. IBEC was prominent along with ICTU in the co-sponsorship of some of these early workplace partnership programmes.

Many of the 'headline' cases used in the promotion of workplace partnership first emerged around this time. Examples include Aughinish Alumina, Aer Rianta, Tegral Metal, AIB and Allianz. Many of these cases survive today while others such as Aer Rianta have ended. Yet other cases such as Lapple Ireland, NEC, Gencorp, and others ended when the owners closed these companies down.

Among these early partnership initiatives were cases that were highly tentative in nature and that involved few issues of any substance. There were, however, also initiatives that were much more confident and that involved wide-ranging and substantial agendas as well as complex structures involving managers, trade union representative and employees at different levels of organisation, Aer Rianta being a case in point. Taken together, these initiatives represented a considerable innovation in Irish industrial relations and change management. Through them, employers and trade union representatives were deliberately seeking to widen the boundaries of the adversarial system and to build relationships aimed at delivering 'mutual gains'. For employers this required that trade unions and employees accepted the necessity for companies to achieve acceptable levels of competitiveness and productivity and the changes needed to ensure this. For employees and unions it required that employers accepted them as legitimate 'stakeholders' in the company with rights to information and consultation as well as rights to share in the benefits of improved company performance.

Such was the interest in these developments and in their North American origins that major US industrial relations scholars were invited to become involved in advice and commentary around the further development of workplace partnership in Ireland. Thomas Kochan of the Massachusetts Institute of Technology (MIT) and co-author of the classic text on partnership, *The Mutual Gains Enterprise* (Kochan and Osterman, 1994), took part in partnership conferences organised by the IPC for companies and trade unions. With Professor Bill Roche he subsequently co-authored a paper for the National Economic and Social Council (NESC) on the development of workplace partnership in Ireland (Roche and Kochan, 1996). The distinguished US political scientist Charles Sabel argued in a report produced for the OECD that there were significant examples of what he termed 'collaborative production' in Irish firms (Sabel, 2006). Robert McKersie, a distinguished scholar at MIT and co-author of the classic text on negotiation theory, *A Behavioural Theory of Labour Negotiation* (Walton and McKersie, 1965) also argued that Ireland represented an ideal context for the development of a new model of employment relations based on partnership between management, employees and unions (McKersie, 1996).

The optimistic view that these partnerships might build in number to become a national model of industrial relations contrasted sharply with the view advanced by Professor Bill Roche that Ireland was experiencing a fragmentation of the adversarial national system of industrial relations into a number of competing systems and that 'divergence' or 'fragmentation' was more likely than the emergence of a new, dominant partnership model.

This book tells the story of the 'first generation' of workplace partnership initiatives that were developed in unionised companies in Ireland in the late 1990s and early 2000s. It is based on doctoral research carried out in the Michael Smurfit Graduate School of Business, University College Dublin in the years 2000-2006. This research constituted the most comprehensive examination of workplace partnerships in Ireland at that time and since. Given the decline in the growth of new cases in the early 2000s it seems reasonable to consider this short period as a distinctive one worthy of examination and commentary. From the vantage point of 2009, these were very much 'pioneering' cases. At the time, management and trade unions had very little experience upon which to draw when designing, implementing and managing these initiatives.

Our main interest in carrying out this research was to explore the workings of what we considered to be 'voluntary' forms of workplace partnership in unionised organisations, i.e. cases where management and trade unions made deliberate decisions to move beyond their adversarial relationships to develop a more cooperative approach to organisational change. We contrast such 'voluntary' partnerships with mandated types such as those found across the public services. In such cases, organisation level partnerships developed for the most part through central agreements rather than through local deliberation. Unlike private companies, management and trade unions in local authorities, health agencies, government departments etc. did not have the facility not to develop partnership arrangements at organisation level.

In this book we seek to answer five main questions: What factors influenced the adoption of workplace partnership? How did the partnerships actually operate? What outcomes did they produce for managers, employees and trade unions? Did they generate so-called 'mutual gains'? Did some types of partnership generate more significant outcomes than others? And, finally, what are the prospects over the coming years of the wider adoption by employers and trade unions of partnership in the workplace?

The book draws on a survey of all known cases of workplace partnership in 2000. The majority of cases were private companies but some cases from the public sector were also included where these had developed out of local decisions in advance of national agreements. The details of this survey and the statistical methods used to analyse the findings are provided in Appendix 1. Because the book is aimed at practitioners as well as scholars and students, we have sought to present some of the more complex statistical tables in a highly simplified format. The research findings are discussed in the context of the theoretical literature on workplace partnership and in the context of other Irish research.

We have used named organisations throughout the text in order to illustrate different aspects of workplace partnership. We have only used cases where public information was available. To protect confidentiality we have not used any information gained through the survey other than in aggregate statistical form. It should not be assumed that the organisations cited in the text participated in the survey.

The book is organised in the following way. Chapter 1 sketches out the development of employee involvement at workplace level in Ireland prior to the formal introduction of workplace partnership in 1997. Chapter 2 outlines how government, employers and trade unions developed workplace partnership through the social partnership arrangements at national level and how they encouraged adoption of this model across the economy. Chapter 3 discusses the research literature on voluntary forms of workplace partnership drawing mainly on North American sources. Chapter 4 describes the main features of the organisations that took part in the survey and reports the findings on the reasons why the organisations concerned adopted partnership. Chapter 5 describes how partnership worked in practice in these organisations, particularly how it was structured and the issues or agendas that were addressed. Chapter 6 outlines the outcomes of partnership for employers, employees and trade unions. Chapter 7 explores how partnership initiatives might be categorised into different types and whether or not different sets of circumstances are likely to lead to the development of different types and whether one type might lead to more significant outcomes than others. Chapter 8 summarises the main findings and discusses their implications for employers, trade unions and policy makers and discusses the prospects for the further development of partnership at workplace level in the private sector.

We owe considerable debts of gratitude to a number of people who have helped us with this and with related work over many years. In particular we are grateful to all the human resource and industrial relations executives who took part in what was a time-consuming and complex survey. Colleagues whose ideas, advice and support we have benefited from include: Tom McGuinness, JJ O'Dwyer, Isobel Butler, Blair Horan, Matt Merrigan, Tom Gormley, Larry Walshe, Kieran Mulvey, John McAdam, Maurice Fines, John O'Halloran, John Dowling, Tim Hastings, Paul Mooney, Jerry Barrett, Stephen McCarthy and Tom Murphy. Professor Bill Roche of UCD has been a constant source of intellectual and moral support over the years. Dr. Teresa Brannick provided extensive and invaluable statistical supports. Enda Hannon provided valuable research assistance in the early stages of the project. Dr. Tim Hastings of the National College of Ireland provided invaluable editorial and moral support. David Givens of The Liffey Press has been a patient and skilful editor. Tom Wall provided useful comments on some sections. As before, this book is dedicated to my wife, Aine O'Neill, and our sons Fintan and Matthew. It is also dedicated to the memories of Kevin Kinsella and Harry Storey.

1

Overview of Employee Involvement

It is generally accepted in the industrialised world that employees should have some level of involvement in the organisational changes that affect their working lives. Employees in Ireland have statutory rights to information and consultation on specific issues such as redundancies. In addition, the Employees (Provision of Information and Consultation) Act 2006 confers rights to information and consultation on competitiveness, work re-organisation, training and development, and employment security but not automatically. There is no automatic entitlement for employees in Ireland to take part in some of the most important organisational changes affecting them such as changes in the structures or operations of their organisations. The issue of how much 'voice' employees should have and how that 'voice' should be expressed is a contested issue between employers and employees. Separate from the 'rights' aspect of employee involvement, many employers accept that there is a strong 'business case' for employee involvement. They consider that employees have a valuable contribution to make based on their knowledge and experience of work processes and work organisation. Many employers also accept that employee understanding of business needs and support for organisational change will be influenced by the degree to which managers foster employee involvement. In this chapter we sketch out the development of employee involvement at workplace level in Ireland prior to the formal introduction of workplace partnership in 1997.

Employee and Trade Union Involvement

Overview of Employee and Trade Union Involvement

The involvement of employees in management decision-making within the workplace has long been a topic of major interest to industrial relations and human resource management scholars and practitioners (Flanders, 1967; Bean, 1994; Hyman and Mason, 1995; Salamon, 2000; Wallace et al., 2004). Managers, trade unions and employees clearly have an interest in employee involvement or participation at workplace level.

Managers require the co-operation of employees with their general goals and strategies. It is widely acknowledged that facilitating employee 'voice' provides a basis for consent and order in the workplace and for reduced levels of conflict (Bean, 1994). Researchers have long concluded that there is an association between workplace relationships and the economic performance of organisations and, indeed, that greater employee and trade union involvement can lead to improved organisational performance (Cutcher-Gershenfeld, 1991; Deery and Iverson, 2005).

Employees, for their part, usually want to have some day-to-day influence on how their work is organised, performed and rewarded. In addition, employees have a broader interest in how their organisations develop because their job security and terms of employment are linked to the success of the organisation. Survey evidence suggests, in fact, that the issues of most concern to union members are not confined to the traditional industrial relations agenda but extend to working in co-operation with management in order to secure the future of their organisations (Geary, 2006).

Trade unions, for their part, recruit members on the basis that organisation will lead to improved pay and conditions and will

give employees some measure of influence over management behaviour and decision-making. They need, therefore, to devise effective ways through which they and their members can achieve
such influence.

The achievement of these varying objectives requires a degree
of recognition, co-operation and involvement by management of
employees and union representatives in the unionised sector
(Freeman and Medoff, 1984; Cradden, 1992; Geraghty, 1992; ICTU,
1993).

Finally, governments as employers of large numbers of staff
and as economic managers and legislators have an interest in the
orderly conduct of industrial relations and in the development of
employee involvement in management decision-making. Employer and trade union bodies seek to influence the direction of
government policy and legislation on employee and trade union
involvement in the workplace.

It might be thought that developing employee involvement
was a straightforward matter. However, employee participation
in decisions in the workplace involves one of the most controversial aspects of employment relationships in advanced industrialised countries. The main reason for this is that it requires managers to involve employees in decisions that traditionally were seen
as being the exclusive prerogative of managers (Hyman and Mason, 1995). Power and control have traditionally been, and continue to be, central dimensions of employee involvement.

Underlying the arguments about employee involvement are
two distinct assumptions about the rights of employers and employees. One assumption is that employees have a right to be part
of the decision-making processes at work in the same way as they
have rights in society generally (Gormley, 2008). On this basis,
trade unions and others have argued for employee and trade union participation on 'industrial democracy' lines.

The other assumption is that employers, as owners, have the
right to determine the form and content of employee and trade

union participation in the workplace (Gormley, 2008). As we have seen, many employers who take this view also take the view that it makes good economic sense to involve employees on workplace issues. Arguments for employee involvement based on democratic rights have been effectively pursued in continental Europe whereas the 'business-based' argument has held sway in the USA (Gormley, 2008). We will see later that these arguments surfaced in Ireland many years ago and continue to surface today.

Much of the management thinking about employee involvement seems to derive from the field of organisational change. Theories of effective change management, especially those associated with 'organisation development' or 'OD', commonly assume that 'ownership' by those affected by changes is vital for success and that such ownership can best be achieved through direct involvement in change processes (Beckhard and Harris, 1977; Kochan and Dyer, 1976). Such involvement, however, is not straightforward because it requires changes in behaviours and attitudes and additional effort from employees and managers (Dundon et al., 2008).

While the literature on organisational change, whether of the 'how to' or academic kind, addresses the role of employees in organisational change it is largely silent on the role of trade unions in workplace change (Kochan and Dyer, 1976; Shirom, 1983; Barling et al., 1992; Merrigan, 2007). This is surprising given that many early applications of OD in the USA took place in unionised settings and were aimed at improving industrial and employee relations (Cummings and Worley, 1997). It is also surprising given the degree of influence that trade unions can have on HR policies and practices, on organisational performance and productivity, on communications and conflict, on changes in organisational structures and cultures, on managerial behaviour and style and so on not to mention more obvious areas such as pay and conditions of employment (Barling et al., 1992). Freeman and Medoff (1984) argue that the behaviour of workers and firms and the outcomes of their interactions differ substantially between the organised and unorganised sectors.

Not taking account of the role of unions in influencing organisational behaviour may lead to the adoption of models of organisational change that are not effective within unionised environments (Kochan and Dyer, 1976). This is an issue to which we will return in the next chapter when discussing the distinctiveness of partnership as an approach to organisational change.

Principal Forms of Employee Involvement

Employers and trade unions have devised a range of ways of involving employees and trade union representatives in workplace issues. The terms 'direct' and 'indirect' or 'representative' are used to distinguish between forms of employee involvement in which individual employees participate 'directly' and forms in which they participate 'indirectly' through trade union representatives. These are summarised in Figure 1.1 below.

Figure 1.1: Direct and Representative Employee Involvement

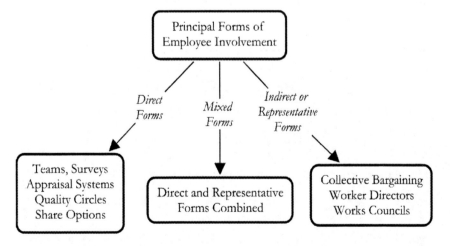

Direct involvement, through teams, surveys, appraisal systems and so on enables employees to have some influence on workplace activities such as how their work is organised and per-formed. There are two broad forms of direct participation, 'con-sultative' and 'delegative', and these may involve individual em-ployees or groups of employees (EFILWC, 1997). In the individual consultative form management retain the right to act or not on suggestions made by individuals, e.g. systematic suggestion schemes and staff attitude surveys. In the individual delegative form employees are given increased discretion and responsibility as individuals to organise and carry out their own work. In the group consultative form there is a permanent group without deci-sion rights, e.g. quality circles where management reserve deci-sion-making authority. Finally, in the group delegative form there is a permanent group with decision rights, e.g. autonomous work groups, often associated with concepts like 'lean production' and 'total quality management'.

Yet another way for employees to become involved is through financial participation in the economic results of a firm's activities (Mason and Hyman, 1995; Cahill, 2000; Pendleton et al., 2001). The most common forms of financial involvement are profit shar-ing which involves employees receiving a variable proportion of their income based on profits; employee share ownership whereby employees own or have the right to own shares (which can be individually or collectively based); and gain sharing which is a group incentive scheme through which employees receive a bonus payment related to the performance of the organisation.

A major survey of direct forms of employee involvement without the participation of trade unions or works councils found that 82 per cent of respondents had some form of direct participa-tion, ranging from 22 per cent with individual consultation to 42 per cent with group delegation and only 10 per cent with multiple forms of direct involvement (EFILWC, 1997). Research has shown that these forms of involvement contribute to positive improve-ments in organisational performance (EFILWC, 1997).

Direct forms of employee involvement have been criticised on the grounds that while they facilitate management communication to employees, they do not provide opportunities for meaningful two-way 'dialogue' that can engage employees in actual decision-making (Dundon et al., 2008). There is an argument that for employees to have a meaningful say, they need to have access not just to information but also to consultation through representative forms of involvement.

Indirect or representative involvement refers to situations where employees use representatives such as shop stewards and full-time union officials to exercise influence on their behalf. The principal way of involving employees through representatives has been collective bargaining, commonly classified as 'adversarial', or industrial relations negotiation. Adversarial collective bargaining is both a method for negotiating wages and conditions of employment and a process for setting the broad contours of the 'social contract' at work, i.e. how managers, union representatives and employees are expected to think about and behave towards each other (Walton et al., 1994). Thus within the 'Anglo Saxon' industrial relations tradition associated with the United Kingdom, the USA, and Ireland, among others, it is assumed that that there is a pervasive conflict of interest between management and trade unions on fundamental issues. This in turn supports a short-term, low trust perspective in which the 'adversarial' strategies and tactics of each side depend on the changing balance of power between them. Kochan (1980) argues that collective bargaining has primary and secondary outcomes for the organisation. Primary outcomes relate to compensation, job security, working conditions, health and safety, industrial relations and human resource policies and practices etc. Secondary outcomes include productivity and performance, turnover, absenteeism, job satisfaction/dissatisfaction, stress, commitment to the organisation and to the union.

There are, however, a number of other forms of indirect participation the broad purpose of which is to reduce conflict and to
improve productivity by giving employees a say in management
decisions. In 'Anglo-Saxon' countries such forms of involvement
have been variously referred to as 'consultation' or 'joint consultation' (Flanders, 1967; Mulvey, 1972). Consultation in Ireland has
traditionally been a voluntary process in which management
seeks the views of employees through their trade union representatives on issues determined by management, in the main produc-
tion-related issues, and with management retaining the discretion
to decide the final outcome. Legislation on redundancies and on
information and consultation provides for employees electing
representatives in situations where there are no trade unions
(Wallace et al., 2004; Faulkner, 2007).

Research has shown that information and consultation
mechanisms can assist in improving workplace relations and the
effectiveness of organisational change and performance in areas
such as workforce flexibility, improved market responsiveness,
adoption of new technology, improved business efficiency, employee business awareness, more co-operative employment relations, and improved product quality and work scheduling (NCPP,
2004 (c); Dundon et al., 2003; Dundon et al., 2008).

Finally, it should be noted that the choices facing employers
and trade unions in terms of selecting methods of employee involvement is not confined to either direct or representative forms.
As our diagram suggests, it is possible to have multiple forms including a mix of direct and representative.

Employee and Trade Union Involvement in Ireland

The Fabric of Industrial Relations in Ireland

Before commencing our discussion of employee involvement in
Ireland it is useful to sketch out some of the industrial relations
context within which employee involvement initiatives have

taken place. Industrial relations in Ireland have typically been characterised as 'adversarial' in terms of overall management-union relations and as 'low' in terms of employee involvement (Murphy and Roche, 1994; Roche, 1996; von Prondzynski, 1996).

The dominant historical influence on Irish industrial relations has been the low trust, adversarial system of the United Kingdom. Collective bargaining has been the dominant approach in resolving workplace disputes, in the introduction of change and in information disclosure (O'Kelly and Doyle, 1997). An important aspect of the British tradition was the idea of an 'auxiliary' role for the state, i.e. one limited to making available publicly funded institutions such as dispute resolution services and basic legislation within which employers and trade unions would settle pay and conditions through free collective bargaining with little interference from government. The key assumption behind this approach was that political stability, economic progress and social peace were best progressed by employers and trade unions with minimal state intervention and through free collective bargaining (Roche and Cradden, 2003).

From the foundation of the state up to the 1950s there was little or no industrial development in Ireland. As late as 1958 there were only 40 companies with more than 500 employees (Kelly and Hourihan, 1997). The focus of collective bargaining appears to have been almost exclusively on wages (O'Mahony, 1964). Managers were reluctant to accord a say to trade unions in workplace decision making on issues outside the traditional bargaining agenda for fear of weakening managerial authority. Trade unions, for their part, were suspicious or even hostile to the direct involvement of their members in management decision-making without the presence of trade union representatives for fear of loss of influence with these members. Where employers desired employee involvement on workplace issues apart from pay and conditions, they had a preference for involving employees directly as individuals rather than through their trade unions.

During this period there appears to have been no widespread interest among employers, trade unions or political parties in extending involvement in management decision-making to employees or trade unions outside of collective bargaining (O'Mahony, 1964). As we have seen, employers and trade unions shared a preference for regulating their own affairs on a 'voluntary' basis rather than through state intervention (Kelly and Hourihan, 1998). There was no ideological disagreement around managerial authority in terms of strategic and commercial decision-making; employees and trade unions accepted for the most part management's 'right to manage' on such issues (Kelly and Hourihan, 1998).

In sum, the prevailing assumption about organisational change was that this was largely a matter for managers to determine with the role of trade unions being largely confined to addressing any implications that changes might have for their members. In the main, unions viewed change as an opportunity to put a price on co-operation in the form of improvements in pay and conditions. In addition, employers and trade unions both wanted to protect existing collective bargaining arrangements and to ensure that these would not be undermined or threatened by new and untested participation systems.

Employee Involvement: The Early Years

In the 1960s industrial growth became a political priority and foreign companies were encouraged to set up operations here (Kelly and Hourihan, 1998). Ireland applied to join the then European Economic Community in 1961 and the government espoused a new policy of free trade as a rejection of earlier failed attempts at self-sufficiency. The initiative to develop representative forms of employee involvement in industry seems to have come from the trade unions when ICTU in 1967 passed a motion calling for 'industrial democracy' providing for worker participation in management. The trade union case for employee participation in the management of companies rested on the industrial democracy argument as well as on arguments of efficiency and industrial peace. ICTU saw participation as an important facility in its own right that helped to strengthen the rights of employees in the workplace and to promote employee satisfaction.

ICTU thinking was based in part on studies of employee participation in the UK, the Federal Republic of Germany, Norway and Yugoslavia. In Northern European countries employee involvement had a statutory basis through 'works councils' and specific workplace issues were subject to 'co-determination' or joint decision-making between management and employees/trade unions (Bean, 1994). Rogers and Streeck (1995) define works councils as institutionalised bodies for representative communications between a single employer and the employees of a single workplace. Works councils represent all the workers and not just those who are unionised. To the extent that representation through works councils and through trade unions are structurally separated, there are two 'channels' of representation available to employees – one through collective bargaining involving trade unions and the other through works councils involving elected employee representatives, usually but not necessarily, trade union nominees.

ICTU recognised at this time that effective employee participation would require the re-organisation of the trade union movement, based as it was on occupational and not industrial grounds. It appears that not all trade unions affiliated to ICTU shared its enthusiasm for industrial democracy.

At this time also, employers began to study industrial democracy. The Federated Union of Employers and the Confederation of Irish Industry (later merged into a single employer body, IBEC) made study visits to the Federal Republic of Germany, the Netherlands, Norway and Yugoslavia. The employer bodies reported to the National Employer-Labour Conference (ELC) in 1970 through the 'Mulvey Report' (Mulvey, 1970). The government had established the ELC in 1962 as a tripartite body representing employers, trade unions and civil servants representing government as employer (Wallace et al., 2004). Employers were less inclined to view participation from an industrial democracy standpoint and were more inclined to consider it as a potential aid in strengthening the identification of employees with the needs of their employers and of increasing levels of support for change.

The Mulvey Report recommended that Ireland not follow the European path of legislating for employee participation through works councils. Instead Mulvey recommended a 'national collective agreement' as the most appropriate and flexible way to promote industrial democracy and argued that legislation would only be appropriate if such an agreement failed (Mulvey, 1972). He also recommended the development on a voluntary basis of a more extensive form of collective bargaining. This would allow for the handling of certain issues, particularly issues such as pay and conditions that were likely to involve conflicting interests, through the traditional adversarial or 'distributive' method of negotiation. It would also allow for the handling of other issues, particularly issues such as organisational change that were likely to involve common interests, through joint problem solving or 'integrative' bargaining.

This formulation presaged by about 25 years the main elements of what was to become known in the 1990s as 'partnership' in the workplace. We will also see later that the thinking behind the Mulvey Report found expression in the national framework agreement on workplace partnership contained in the national programme, *Partnership 2000*.

In 1974 an ELC sub-committee issued a discussion document that concluded that works councils would benefit individual enterprises and the economy and that the best way of achieving employee participation was through a national collective agreement covering the private and public sectors (Department of Labour, 1986). The form that works councils would take would be a matter for local discussion. This appeared to satisfy the position of the trade unions in favour of works councils and the position of the employers in favour of a voluntary rather than a statutory approach to participation.

The sub-committee had concerns that the expansion of employee participation might be hindered by inadequate trade union resources and by the low priority given to personnel management by senior managers. The ELC did not ratify the sub-committee report. ICTU supported its provisions in general terms. However, the report is important as the first effort by a joint working group of the social partners to develop a joint national position on employee participation (Department of Labour, 1986). Thus we can see as early as the 1970s the different policies of employers and trade unions on the 'statutory-voluntary' and 'direct-representative' questions that still dominate, as we will see later, debates among employers and trade unions on employee involvement in the workplace.

Joint Consultation through Works Committees

In 1973, the FIE and ICTU agreed a draft declaration on employee involvement at workplace level that was meant to appear in the third National Wage Agreement. It was never ratified because the priorities of employers and trade unions changed in light of the first OPEC oil crisis and subsequent global recession (O'Kelly and Doyle, 1997). It appears, nevertheless, that there was some development of 'joint consultation' in Ireland during the 1970s. Joint consultation was defined as the organisation of committees or councils composed of representatives of management and employees, which meet to consider various company activities but excluding meetings of a collective bargaining type. Typical names for such groups included 'joint consultation committee', 'works committee', 'works council' and 'joint productivity committee'.

A 1976 study by the former IPC based on a survey of managers found that about one-third of the 490 manufacturing companies that responded to the survey currently had some form of 'joint consultation' (Hanlon, 1976). Firms of 100 or more employees were twice as likely to have joint consultation as firms of 50-99 employees. Almost seven out of ten companies (68 per cent) said that they had established their joint consultation systems in the years 1970-75. In 70 per cent of cases the joint consultation system was a management initiative and in 63 per cent of cases the system was agreed with the trade unions concerned. In roughly half of the cases employee representatives had to be union members.

Agendas focused on four categories of issues, viz welfare/social, working conditions, union matters and company/business productivity. Almost all respondents (98 per cent) perceived the joint consultation arrangements as being useful in running the companies concerned. However, only 25 per cent reported that the arrangements had 'helped greatly' while 51 per cent considered them to have been 'useful to some extent'. Joint consultation had the most effect on reducing grievances, improving amenities, improving morale, creating a better understanding of workers' problems by management, and on improving industrial relations. Joint consultation had the least impact on absenteeism and time-keeping, on production methods and on quality of work. There were no findings relating to outcomes for employees or trade unions. Contemporary and later commentators have tended to dismiss these examples of joint consultation as of little significance (Mulvey, 1972; McCarthy, 1975; Kelly and Hourihan, 1998). A much later survey of joint consultative committees found that 25 per cent of respondents had joint consultative committees or works councils – 38 per cent in the public sector, 21 per cent in the private sector – and with the majority having been established more than three years previously (Gunnigle et al., 1997).

Worker Directors and Sub-Board Structures

In the 1970s employee involvement became a political issue with Fianna Fáil, Labour and Fine Gael all adopting detailed policies on the development of employee participation (Department of Labour, 1986). In 1977 a Fine Gael–Labour Party Coalition introduced the Worker Participation (State Enterprises) Act. This provided for the election of worker representatives, who would have the same independent status as other board members, to one-third of the seats on the boards of seven state enterprises. Representation at board level opened up the possibility of workers having an influence on strategic decision-making. The Worker Participation (State Enterprises) Act 1988 subsequently added seven more state enterprises. The introduction of this legislation had been provided for in the 1987 *Programme for National Recovery* (Government of Ireland, 1987), which was the first of the current series of 'national programmes'. In addition, the legislation provided that board-level participation could be extended to other state companies without further legislation (Wallace et al., 2004). The right to nominate candidates was confined to trade unions or other staff organisations that were recognised for collective bargaining purposes.

It was hoped by the framers of the legislation that this innovation would facilitate the involvement of employees at sub-board levels and that it would provide a headline that other sectors would follow. In the years since the passage of the original legislation it became apparent that few sub-boards structures had been developed in the state companies (Kelly and Hourihan, 1997). Consequently, the 1988 legislation provided for the establishment of 'sub-board structures' and identified 39 state companies in which this might happen. State financial institutions such as the Central Bank and others were excluded from the provisions for reasons of confidentiality.

The legislation left it to management and/or employees and their representatives to initiate discussions and to agree acceptable arrangements that could involve direct and/or representative forms of a highly structured or informal kind (Kelly and Hourihan, 1997). The purpose of the sub-board structures was to facilitate the exchange of views and information between the companies and their employees, the communication of information likely to have a significant effect on employees, and the distribution of views and information arising from the participatory process to all employees (Wallace et al., 2004). It was estimated that some 28 companies had established sub-board structures by 1997 (Kelly and Hourihan, 1997).

A number of reviews support some broad conclusions as to the impact of the legislation on worker directors and sub-board structures. Reviews of the operation of worker directors concluded that the experience had been broadly successful for the worker directors and for senior management, that the system had not led to conflicts with the operations of the trade unions or of collective bargaining, and that employees had a positive response to board level representation (Wallace et al., 2004). Shop stewards were positively disposed towards worker directors but were sceptical about the degree of influence that they might have at board level given their minority position. Full time union officials were sceptical of the capacity of worker directors to contribute to improvements in industrial relations. Both shop stewards and full time officials considered that they had a greater capacity than worker directors to resolve problems affecting employees in the workplace (Kelly and Hourihan, 1997). There were clearly tensions, then, among the trade union actors around the new role of worker director and how it might affect their members' perceptions of the role of shop stewards and full time officials.

Worker directors considered that they had been effective in bringing attention to the needs of employees in board decision-making, in influencing better communications between the board and employees and in bringing considerable industrial relations competence to board deliberations (Kelly and Hourihan, 1997). Worker directors identified the main challenges they encountered as: making an impact on board decision-making, overcoming hostility and suspicion among other board members and senior management, handling confidentiality on issues affecting the workforce, mastering technical and financial information, and being excluded from key board sub-committees. Worker directors were careful not to offend union-company negotiations and communications (Kelly and Hourihan, 1997).

The reviews did not throw light on the effects, if any, that worker directors and sub-board structures, might have had on organisational performance. The example of worker directors in the state sector did not lead to private sector employers taking initiatives along similar lines.

Today, several of these state companies such as eircom and Aer Lingus are now in private ownership. The remaining state companies still have worker directors and many also have sub-board structures. In 2002, the LRC carried out a review of the Worker Participation (State Enterprises) Acts, 1977 and 1988. The objective of the review was to inform decisions affecting the future of worker directors in the context of the sale of any semi-state companies covered by the legislation. The review noted that IBEC and ICTU had diametrically opposing views as to what arrangements should apply in such cases. Employers argued against further legislation and for a voluntary approach while unions argued for extending the statutory basis of employee involvement in such cases. The review concluded that the overall impact of the legislation had been positive in that having worker directors and sub-board structures had helped to foster more co-operative relationships and had contributed to the development of the companies concerned. The review referred the issue of the future of worker directors in the context of the sale of any semi-state companies back to the social partners for further discussion.

Development of New Forms of Employee Involvement in the 1980s

Another significant development during the 1980s was the introduction of various forms of employee involvement under the general heading of 'new forms of work organisation'. This included
the establishment by employers of semi-autonomous work groups
to which management would delegate varying degrees of responsibility for aspects of work organisation. It appears that these
forms of direct employee involvement were developed to elicit
greater employee involvement in the solution of production-
related problems rather than to empower employees per se (Bean,
1994). The development of these new forms of employee involvement has been associated with a shift in the 'centre of grav-
ity' of industrial relations in many advanced economies away
from the state towards individual organisations, away from trade
unions towards employers, and away from adversarial industrial
relations towards a more strategy-related employee relations
model termed 'human resource management' or 'HRM' (Regini,
1995; Ferner and Hyman, 1994; Locke et al., 1995). These studies
relate this shift to severe economic crisis and the emergence of a
'new competitive order' that influenced the development by firms
of new forms of work organisation that were less hierarchical,
more flexible, and less in need of low-skilled than high-skilled
employees who would be capable of taking on responsibility for
issues such as quality and maintenance which previously would
have been the preserve of specialists or supervisors.

Among the innovations that emerged were, on the one hand,
initiatives by employers and governments to deregulate the employment relationship and to apply non-union 'HRM' practices
and, on the other hand, initiatives by employers to develop more
co-operative management-union relations. The latter approach
provided for employee participation in the form of semi-
autonomous groups, teams, quality circles and other 'high involvement' work practices such as 'total quality management'

which increased employee responsibility for the organisation of work. In the 1960s, many US companies agreed to recognise trade unions on the advice of the then Industrial Development Authority, the state body charged with attracting foreign companies. However, since the 1980s this has changed and today American multinationals, as well as others, are increasingly unlikely to recognise trade unions in new manufacturing plants in Ireland (Wallace et al., 2004; Lavelle et al., 2008).

Trade unions in the private sector responded positively, at least in policy terms, to these initiatives. ICTU produced two seminal reports that set out how trade unions might collaborate with employers to secure the prosperity of enterprises while advancing their own interests at the same time (ICTU, 1993 and 1995). These reports acknowledged the limitations of the dominant adversarial model of industrial relations for both employers and trade unions. These reports reflected a 'modernising' leadership in ICTU and a thawing of trade union opposition to direct forms of employee involvement and HRM as management approaches that were assumed to be hostile to trade union interests (Cradden, 1992).

A number of studies have examined the incidence of 'new forms of work organisation' (McCartney and Teague, 1998; Gunnigle et al., 1997; Roche and Geary, 1998; Geary, 1999). McCartney and Teague (1997) concluded that there was a relatively high overall incidence of these practices with two-thirds of respondents using 'total quality management', a majority using job rotation, almost half having at least one quality circle, and more than a quarter using team working. Geary (1999) concluded that changes in work reorganisation were certainly taking place in many companies in Ireland but that work reorganisation of a substantial kind was only taking place in a minority of cases. In addition, three factors emerged as having a strong influence on the adoption of these new work practices. These were 'high tech' companies, financial services and competitive strategies that emphasised product and service customisation (Geary, 1999). As with other forms of employee involvement, the international and Irish research shows positive company performance outcomes resulting from 'new forms of work organisation' and 'high performance work systems' (Ichniowski et al., 1996; NCPP, 2008).

The EU Directive on Information and Consultation

The 2002 EU Directive on Information and Consultation was transposed into Irish law through The Employees (Provision of Information and Consultation) Act 2006. Since March 2008, the legislation has created an employee right to information and consultation in undertakings with at least 50 employees. The term 'undertaking' means a public or private organisation carrying out an economic activity whether operating for gain or not. Thus the legislation applies to the private sector and parts of the public sector, including health and local government but not, apparently, the civil service. The types of information envisaged include information about the undertaking's activities and economic situation, about the probable development of employment within the undertaking and any measures envisaged where there is a threat to employment, and about decisions likely to lead to substantial changes in work organisation or in contractual relations.

Employers may voluntarily propose information and consultation mechanisms to their employees and/or their representatives. Employers may propose 'direct' forms of information and consultation or they may propose mixing direct and representative forms as long as employees agree to this. Alternatively at least 10 per cent of the employees (with a minimum of 15 or 30 per cent in the case of organisations with 50 employees) or their representatives may 'trigger' negotiations through a written request. In effect, then, the legislation does not confer an automatic right to employee information and consultation. If employers or employees do not 'trigger' the legislation then it does not come into effect.

Trade unions are not the sole channel for employee representation under the new legislation or under the original EU Directive. Employees may elect or appoint whomsoever they choose to
be their representatives or they may choose to become involved
directly rather than through representatives. Where trade unions
are recognised for collective bargaining negotiations they are enti-
tled to have representation for the purposes of the legislation.

It appears that ICTU favoured the negotiation of a national
framework agreement on the implementation of the Information
and Consultation Directive but that IBEC did not (Wall, 2004;
Geary and Roche, 2005). IBEC and ICTU had separate discussions
with the Department of Enterprise, Trade and Employment
(DETE). The American Chamber of Commerce, representing large
US multinationals, seems to have had a significant influence on
the legislation (IRN, 28 July 2005). The legislation, according to
DETE, reflects the need to balance the competing demands of employers, development agencies and trade unions (IRN, 28 March
2007).

Broadly speaking, IBEC appeared satisfied with the legislation
whereas ICTU expressed strong dissatisfaction (IRN, 26 July
2006). The most controversial aspect of the new legislation for IC-
TU was that it did not apply automatically but had to be 'trig-
gered'. Unions also saw the provisions for 'direct' as well as 'representative' forms as concessions to the IBEC position.

Before its enactment, the legislation was described as the single greatest innovation in Irish employment relations in recent
times (Geary and Roche, 2005) and as having potential to lead to
the greater diffusion of partnership (IRN, 7 July 2005). It now appears, however, that the directive has been transposed in a manner likely to severely limit its impact. Apart from some headline
cases, the level of uptake appears extremely low.

There does not appear to be much activity among employers
or trade unions around the new legislation (IRN, 28 March 2007).
The only cases to date where the Labour Court became involved

were in the public service where the Court found that the HSE had breached the legislation (IRN, 27 February 2008). In 2008 the Department of Enterprise Trade and Employment published a code of practice on information and consultation that had been prepared by the LRC (DETE, 2008).

Explaining the Limited Development of Employee Involvement up to the 1990s

Before completing our overview of the development of employee involvement in Ireland by addressing the development of 'workplace partnership' in the next chapter, we will consider how to explain the limited development of employee involvement up to the 1990s.

One line of explanation can be found in Ireland's economy. This was largely farming-based up to the 1960s and significant industrial development only began to take place in the 1970s. This meant that the number of companies of a sufficiently large size to warrant formal arrangements for employee consultation was quite small during this period. Another line of explanation relates to the traditional low trust, adversarial industrial relations tradition that discouraged the open sharing of information between management, employees and trade unions.

Another line of explanation relates to the characteristics of management and trade unions. As early as the 1970s, commentators were critical of the capability of personnel managers and of trade unions to manage employee involvement systems. The multiplicity of unions made dealing with them outside of collective bargaining an unattractive prospect for employers (Kelly and Hourihan, 1997). It has also been argued that trade unions in Ireland lacked the resources and expertise to break from the adversarial industrial relations tradition (Geary, 1999). In addition, unions had fears that a formal representative system based on elected employees might supplant the union in the negotiation of collective agreements (Kelly and Hourihan, 1997). Until the 1980s most trade unions in Ireland showed little interest in becoming involved in workplace changes such as new forms of work organisation that had potential to advance the employee participation agenda (ICTU, 1993; Kelly and Hourihan, 1997; Geary, 1999).

Another line of explanation may be found in the 'weak' or 'auxiliary' role of the Irish state, i.e. interfering as little as possible in industrial relations and leaving employers and trade unions to manage their own affairs within a general legislative framework (Roche, 1997). One of the most important factors hindering the wider development of employee involvement was the absence of any consensus between employers and trade unions on the role of employee involvement in the workplace. Employers, as we have seen, have always sought to protect managerial prerogative and have advocated a voluntary company-by-company approach to employee participation (Kelly and Hourihan, 1997). They have also advocated direct as opposed to representative forms of involvement. Unions, as we have seen, favoured representative forms of involvement and a statutory approach where possible. While Irish governments were sympathetic to the appeals of trade unions for greater employee involvement in the workplace they were not willing to ignore the views of employers.

We saw that the dominant early influence on industrial relations in Ireland was the UK adversarial system. There appears to have been a weakening of the UK influence in the 1970s when Ireland became influenced by wider developments around employee participation in Western Europe, particularly Germany and the Scandinavian countries (Bean, 1994). Ireland's membership of the EEC and later European Union (EU) had a significant positive influence on the development of employee involvement, including the introduction of the information and consultation legislation as well as legislation guaranteeing employee involvement in decisions relating to redundancies. The development of a strong multinational sector including many US companies also had a significant influence. Many multinationals practiced direct forms of employee involvement such as teams and new forms of work organisation.

Summary and Conclusions

In this chapter we have seen that Ireland had a 'weak' tradition of employee involvement in workplace decision-making. Employee involvement has always been a contested issue between employers and trade unions. Employers favoured direct forms of involvement while trade unions favoured indirect or representative forms. Unions favoured a statutory approach while employers favoured a voluntary one. From the 1970s onwards, the main pressure for increased forms of representative involvement came from the trade unions. Key developments in the history of employee involvement included voluntary works councils in the 1970s, worker directors and sub-board structures in state companies in the 1980s, direct forms of employee involvement under the heading of 'new forms of work organisation' in the 1980s, and legislation for employee information and consultation in 2006. In the next chapter we will outline in detail how employers and trade unions agreed on a new national framework for the development of 'workplace partnership' through the national social partnership arrangements.

2

WORKPLACE PARTNERSHIP IN CONTEXT

In this chapter we outline how employers and trade unions developed workplace partnership through the social partnership arrangements at national level. We identify partnership as a distinctive approach to organisational change and outline the initiatives that employers, trade unions and government took to encourage adoption of this model across the economy. We argue that this form of employee and trade union involvement was the most advanced form developed to date in Ireland. We provide some examples of workplace partnership in action and we discuss the extent to which it has developed since the late 1990s when first introduced through the national programme, *Partnership 2000*.

Negotiating Employee Involvement through Social Partnership

Since 1986 Irish governments, IBEC and ICTU negotiated seven multi-year agreements on pay and social and economic issues. Over the years, in addition to solving problems through traditional 'hard bargaining', the parties developed what was later called a 'joint problem solving' approach (O'Donnell and O'Reardon, 2000). Typically this approach involved joint working groups that gathered and analysed data and that sought mutually acceptable outcomes from among a range of options. This 'partnership' approach, as it later became know, was considered a key factor in the emergence of the 'Celtic Tiger' economy (Wallace et al., 2004; Hastings et al., 2007).

Not surprisingly, the national negotiation agenda included employee and trade union involvement (Wall, 2004). Figure 2.1 summarises the employee involvement elements of these national programmes.

Figure 2.1 National Programmes and Employee Involvement

Programme	Employee Involvement Elements
1987: Programme for National Recovery (PNR)	• Enabling legislation to facilitate sub-board structures in state enterprises • Discussions on better framework for negotiation and dispute settlement
1991: Programme for Economic and Social Progress (PESP)	• Monitor introduction of sub-board structures in state enterprises • FIE and ICTU to publish joint declaration on employee involvement
1994: Programme for Competitive-ness and Work (PCW)	• IBEC/ICTU Joint Declaration on Employee Involvement • Agreement to promote employee involvement • IPC as 'national participation agency'
1997: Partnership 2000	• Chapter 9 Action through Partnership for Competitive Enterprises • Modernising industrial relations • Chapter 10 Action to Modernise the Public Service • National Centre for Partnership (NCP)
2000: Programme for Prosperity and Fairness (PPF)	• Continuation of Chapter 9 and Chapter 10 arrangements from Partnership 2000 • NCP becomes National Centre for Partnership and Performance (NCPP) on statutory basis
2003: Sustaining Progress (SP)	• Actions from NCPP • Publication of Review of Worker Participation (State Enterprises) Acts, 1977 and 1988
2006: Towards 2016 (T16)	• Report on Workplace of the Future • Workplace Innovation Fund
2008: Transitional Agreement (TA)	• NCPP activities agreed

In the first national programme, the *Programme for National Recovery* (Government of Ireland, 1987), references to employee participation were confined to state enterprises, as we saw earlier. There was also an agreement to discuss a better framework for collective bargaining and dispute settlement that would support employment-generating investment, reflecting a common concern among the social partners that workplace industrial relations should facilitate organisational change.

In 1991 the *Programme for Economic and Social Progress* (Government of Ireland, 1991) stated that the then Federation of Irish Employers and ICTU would publish a joint declaration on employee involvement in the private sector. In 1994 the *Programme for Competitiveness and Work* (Government of Ireland, 1994) acknowledged the IBEC/ICTU joint declaration and stressed the importance of employee involvement for competitiveness, job satisfaction, and closer identification of employees with their companies. The agreement committed the social partners to promoting the voluntary adoption at local level of information sharing/communications/consultation programmes, consultation through representative mechanisms, financial involvement, quality of working life programmes and involvement groups/quality circles. The agreement also emphasised the importance of changes in the production process, in work organisation, in working conditions and in industrial relations to realise the potential for job creation arising from new technologies. There was also agreement to support the work of the IPC as the 'national participation agency'.

The most significant national programme in terms of employee involvement was without doubt *Partnership 2000* (Government of Ireland, 1997). In this agreement the social partners made the development of 'partnership' a central and common objective in both the private and public sectors. This programme identified partnership with the attainment of goals such as competitiveness and improved quality of the work environment in the private sector and with 'modernisation' in the public services. It established a 'national framework' for developing partnership and put supports in place including a National Centre for Partnership (NCP). While the impetus towards greater employee involvement had primarily come from the private sector unions, there was an equal emphasis on this from the public service unions in the negotiations leading to *Partnership 2000* (Wall, 2004; Merrigan, 2007). The public service unions had seen examples of partnership at work in the private sector and considered that it might provide a suitable mechanism for involvement in the public services, something that had become important in the context of changes under the public service 'modernisation' programmes.

Partnership was presented as a more co-operative approach to industrial relations and organisational change. Partnership was defined as (Government of Ireland, 1997; 62):

> an active relationship based on a common interest to secure the competitiveness and prosperity of the enterprise. It involves a commitment by employees to improvements in quality and efficiency; and the acceptance by employers of employees as stakeholders with rights and interests to be considered in the context of major decisions affecting their employment. Partnership provides for direct participation of employees/representatives and investment in training, development and the working environment.

The definition is deliberately vague to allow for partnership in unionised and non-union employments. It also allows for direct as well as representative forms of involvement (ICTU, 1997; IBEC, 1998). *Partnership 2000* did not attempt to impose any single structure or model of partnership. Rather it noted the need to tailor approaches to fit different employment settings. Indeed, the social partners appeared at pains to point out that there was no one model of partnership that was applicable in all circumstances and that there was no evidence that any one structural model systematically out-performed others (NESC, 1996, 1999). The agreement encouraged firms, employees and unions to experiment and to develop new models of involvement. It acknowledged that for some employers, employees, and union representatives, partnership would require a radical change in current attitudes and approaches. The agreement represented a significant step on the part of employers and trade unions in that they committed themselves not just to a single 'guiding vision' of public policy on employment relations (Roche, 2006(a)) but also to active support for the development of workplace partnership both separately and together.

The agreement on workplace partnership was no doubt helped by the fact that IBEC and ICTU were working together on a number of EU-funded projects on the development of workplace partnership, including joint training programmes for management and trade union representatives (Totterdill and Sharpe, 1999; Healy, 2000). In the years 1996 to 2000 some forty companies participated in the different EU-funded projects initiated by IBEC, ICTU, IPC and SIPTU. The partnership elements in *Partnership 2000* represented a significant achievement for ICTU and the 'modernising' strategy that it had developed over the previous number of years.

Partnership 2000 set out broad agenda headings including competitiveness, training, equality of opportunities, representational arrangements, financial involvement, health and safety, the work environment, composition of the workforce, co-operation with change including new forms of work organisation, problem solving and conflict avoidance, and adaptability, flexibility and innovation. The agreement stressed that negotiations would take place 'in a non-adversarial manner' (Government of Ireland, 1997; 53). It noted that a big challenge for companies and unions would be to move from the traditional approach to the organisation of work to more flexible work practices, to strike a balance between flexibility and security and to develop a high trust environment between employees and managers. As noted in the last chapter, the new agreement constituted a 'national framework' as envisaged in the 1972 Mulvey Report and provided for a separation

between the handling of issues through traditional industrial relations and the new, more co-operative partnership arrangements.

Trade unions and employers subsequently engaged in 'chapter nine' negotiations at a local level and reached agreements that
provided for a wide range of organisational changes as well as for
pay increases, including some 'gain-sharing' arrangements, and
for the establishment of different forms of partnership bodies
(IRN, 16 December 1999). SIPTU made a point of seeking the establishment of partnership forums as part of their local bargaining
strategy (IRN, 29 October 1998). Twelve out of 48 local agreements that were reviewed involved the setting up of some form of
partnership forum or consultative body (IRN, 16 December 1999).
New partnership bodies included 'steering groups' and representative 'partnership forums' charged with developing specific improvement initiatives as well as partnership in general.

In 2000 in the *Programme for Prosperity and Fairness* (Government of Ireland, 2000) the social partners continued the arrangements set out in *Partnership 2000* for partnership in the private and
public sectors. They put the NCP on a statutory basis as the National Centre for Partnership and Performance (NCPP) with Peter
Cassells, former general secretary of ICTU as executive chairper-
son. In 2003 in *Sustaining Progress* (Government of Ireland, 2003)
the parties established a 'Forum on the Workplace of the Future'
under the NCPP. They also agreed to publish an LRC review of
the Worker Participation (State Enterprises) Acts, 1977 and 1988.
We discussed the review in the last chapter.

The NCPP published a valuable series of research reports on
partnership and related matters (see www.ncpp.ie). The government and its agencies as well as the national employer and trade
union bodies, IBEC and ICTU, encouraged the diffusion of workplace partnership through policy statements as well as through
practical supports (Government of Ireland, 1997; ICTU, 1997;
IBEC, 1998). The promotional activities carried out under these
programmes represented a significant effort on the part of the so-

cial partners to promote partnership. With hindsight, this period probably represented a high water mark in terms of active collaboration between IBEC and ICTU.

Sustaining Progress committed government to transpose the 2002 EU Directive on Information and Consultation into Irish law by March 2005 although, as seen in the last chapter, this did not happen on time. In *Towards 2016* the government agreed to establish a 'workplace innovation fund' to support innovation and partnership (Government of Ireland, 2006). In the *Transitional Agreement* (Government of Ireland, 2008) the role of the NCPP in developing policy on change management was confirmed (IRN, 23 September 2008).

Partnership: A Step Forward from Earlier Forms of Employee Involvement

A number of factors seemed to distinguish partnership from earlier forms of employee involvement. The proposed involvement of trade unions in the design and operation of partnership systems differentiated these from earlier forms of employee involvement (Roche and Geary, 2006). While earlier initiatives tended to emphasise direct forms of involvement, *Partnership 2000* explicitly referred to both representative and direct forms. It appeared that partnership had the potential to meet the democratic needs of workers and unions for input into managerial decision-making while accommodating employer needs for competitiveness (Gormley, 2008). While partnership was not put on a statutory footing there was a statutory body, the NCPP, responsible for its promotion and partnership became, as indicated earlier, the guiding vision for public policy on employment relations.

The term 'partnership' and the promotion of joint management-union training suggested a willingness on the part of private sector employers to acknowledge a positive role for trade unions in workplace decision-making. However, the term 'partnership' has over the years become quite vague in its definition and has been used to describe a range of 'positive' employee relations practices in both the union and non-union sectors (NCPP, 2008).

It is important to note that the development of workplace partnership was not the only aspect of employee involvement that was the subject of negotiation over this series of national programmes. In the late 1990s the issue of trade union recognition became a central concern at social partnership discussions (IRN, 3 February 2000). ICTU sought to build on EU developments that provided for the development of representation and recognition rights in respect to collective redundancies, transfer of undertakings, health and safety, information and consultation rights etc. ICTU argued for statutory trade union recognition. IBEC strongly opposed this. IBEC argued for retaining the traditional 'voluntarist' approach to industrial relations and insisted that different companies had the right to decide what approaches to employee relations were appropriate to their particular circumstances, including the role accorded or not accorded to trade unions.

The negotiations on trade union recognition led to the Industrial Relations Amendment Acts (2001 and 2004). This legislation provided procedures for resolving workplace disputes where negotiating arrangements were not in place and where the parties were not engaged in talks. The unions argued that the 2007 Supreme Court 'Ryanair Judgment' which established that collective bargaining could take place through alternative bodies to trade unions undermined the new legislation and Labour Court role. IBEC took the view that the Labour Court had defined collective bargaining too narrowly and that the judgment had been a necessary corrective to this. They argued that collective bargaining should not be defined in a manner that would prejudice the right of non-union companies to maintain their own internal arrangements for collective bargaining (IRN, 8 May 2008). This case has been described as one of the most significant legal decisions of recent years (Gilvarry and Hunt, 2008). Hence, the recognition issue has come back on the agenda (IRN, 1 May 2007 and 17 September 2008).

Partnership as an Approach to Organisational Change – Beyond Adversarialism

How can we differentiate partnership as an approach to organisational change from other approaches? Perhaps the most distinctive feature of partnership is the role of trade unions. We saw in the last chapter that most of the writing on organisational change ignores the role of trade unions. In Ireland there are some notable exceptions in recent studies of Aer Rianta (Roche and Geary, 2006), ESB, eircom, An Post, Aer Lingus (Hastings, 2003), Waterford Glass and Aughinish Alumina (Dobbins, 2008).

There are three broad aspects of unionised organisations that need to be taken into account in the design of change initiatives – goals, power and conflict (Kochan and Dyer, 1976). Management and employees generally share goals or interests around the growth and prosperity of the organisation. They may, however, have conflicting goals around how changes should be implemented or around how the benefits of growth should be divided. When this happens, employees who are union members turn to the union to help achieve these goals. The union, in turn, has goals or interests around recognition, membership growth, having influence over decision-making and so on. In unionised organisations neither the employer nor the union has absolute power over the other; power is shared through the collective bargaining process. Conflict, then, is structurally based in that it results from the fact that parties inevitably have different goals or interests that need to be resolved (Kochan and Dyer, 1976).

It is not surprising, then, that *Partnership 2000* acknowledges the legitimacy of the differences in goals between employers, employees and trade unions and balances management goals or interests such as competitiveness, employee flexibility and co-operation with change, with employee goals or interests such as financial involvement, health and safety, training and development, quality of the working environment etc. The essence of partnership is that management, employees and trade unions strive to work together to solve problems through cooperation, as opposed to engaging in conflict and adversarialism (Gunnigle et al., 2004).

Most managerial writing on change management assumes that there is only one organisation, i.e. the employing organisation, and that consequently there is only one set of goals or interests to be taken into account in the change process. A partnership approach assumes that change management is a negotiated process and not one that can be directed by management alone (Walton et al, 1994). Partnership structures provide the parties with mechanisms through which they can be active in advancing their legitimate and sometimes conflicting interests.

In so far as partnership provides for management, employees and trade unions working together on agreed change initiatives, it seems reasonable to call it a 'planned' approach to change. Partnership shares much in common with the classic 'planned' approach to organisational change, i.e. 'organisation development' or 'OD' (Cummings and Worley, 1997; Coghlan and McAuliffe, 2003). This is not surprising given that the roots of OD in the USA include team building, action research, participative management, productivity and the quality of working life, and strategic change (Cummings and Worley, 1997). OD emphasises the planned nature of change, change as a process that needs to be understood and managed, the importance of manager and employee involvement, team building, conflict management, staff representation and joint problem identification, trust building, action learning, and the importance of the role of 'change agent' or facilitator (Coghlan and McAuliffe, 2003; IBEC, 2008).

The pursuit through partnership of more co-operative industrial and employee relations and of 'continuous improvement' practices may be seen as an example of the type of 'culture' change often associated with OD (Coghlan and McAuliffe, 2003; Totterdill and Sharpe, 1999). In sum, then, it seems reasonable to argue that partnership, as articulated in *Partnership 2000*, is not simply an attempt to adjust the climate of industrial and employee relations in organisations but represents a distinctive model of organisational change in the unionised sector in Ireland.

In the language of 'strategic negotiations', partnership is a 'fostering' strategy aimed at developing high commitment among employees and a more co-operative relationship with the union as a basis for developing more effective organisations. It seeks voluntary employee and trade union participation in change as opposed to mere compliance with change. It contrasts with 'forcing' strategies through which employers seek to push through changes even at the expense of working relationships with employees and their union representatives (Walton et al., 1994).

Examples of Workplace Partnership

In Exhibits 1 and 2 we outline two of the partnerships that received early public attention and which endure to this day – Allied Irish Banks (IRN 7: 17 February 2000; 16: 17 April 2003; 44: 17 November 2005) and Tegral Metal-Forming Ltd (NCPP, 2003; IRN, 26: 11 July 2007).

The AIB/IBOA partnership developed in the wake of a bitter industrial dispute that left relationships at an all-time low. In many such cases, employers and trade unions take a fatalistic approach and 'leave well enough alone'. In this instance the parties decided to act on the problem rather than to let it fester in the hope that it might improve over time.

Tegral Metal Forming Ltd (TMF) was established in 1977 in Athy, Co. Kildare. It employed 80 people in 2002. Its main activities are cold steel forming, and supplying steel roofing, cladding and flooring products mainly for the Irish market. The two cases illustrate the different contexts in which partnership can be developed, the range of issues that can be addressed and the different structures that management and trade unions can employ in order to engage with each other at different levels of organisation.

The AIB case highlights a 'top down' approach to partnership with active involvement from senior leaders on both sides and with little early involvement by managers, employees or union representatives at operational levels. This case also shows how employers and trade unions can plan and manage their partnership and industrial relations agendas – pay, working hours and organisational change – in a creative manner, in this case through an externally facilitated tribunal.

The TMF case highlights the pattern followed in many partnerships that were developed through the various EU-funded projects, viz a combination of strategic and operational level groups providing for wide involvement at different levels of organisation, active external facilitation and an agenda comprising of issues of particular value to management such as productivity improvements and of particular value to employees such as gain-sharing.

Exhibit 1.1: Allied Irish Banks

In 1994, in the wake of a bitter dispute, the management and the union – Irish Bank Officials' Association (IBOA) – agreed to develop a better way of doing business than the prevailing adversarial approach. They formed a six-person 'joint working party' that included high-level leaders on both sides. The group worked without any external assistance. Work began on a range of significant change issues such as new banking services and new opening hours, as well as on a new working relationship and more efficient industrial relations. The parties agreed that there must be 'no surprises' as far as possible. Two years later management and union agreed a set of principles to guide their relationships: enhancing the prosperity of the organisation; maintaining secure employment; raising levels of trust; acknowledging employees' right to join a union and recognition of IBOA; developing a co-operative culture through agreed adaptability, flexibility and innovation; and creating a structure which gives effect to true partnership. In 2003 they announced a 'milestone' agreement on pay, working hours and organisational changes. They accredited the achievement of this progress to a new tribunal agreed through the partnership. In 2005 Peter Cassells, now chair of their 'partnership steering committee', facilitated a review of the AIB/IBOA partnership. As a result, they decided to form a closer link between the industrial relations agenda and the strategic priorities of the business within the partnership, to include local managers and representatives in partnership activity, to further develop their industrial relations procedures, and to develop joint communications. The emphasis of what they termed their new 'second generation partnership' was to be on 'mutual gains' – facilitating the management of change to improve performance and addressing how staff can share in the benefits.

Exhibit 1.2: Tegral Metal-Forming Ltd.

In 1996/97, the management and unions - SIPTU and TEEU – agreed to take part in the IPC's 'New Work Organisation Programme'. An overall 'partnership forum' was established with management and union representatives including full time union officials. In addition, there was a ' steering committee'. The IPC provided external facilitation and support including joint management-union training. A number of ground-level 'task teams' were also established to address specific issues including how to handle scrap metal and introducing a new IT system. While industrial relations issues were to be handled separately, the practice has been that some issues were resolved through the 'task teams'. Because of the success of these initiatives, management and unions decided to develop a team-based structure on a pilot basis in one part of the plant. A 'gain-sharing' scheme formed part of the pilot. Where difficulties arose in the ground-level partnership groups these were referred up to the 'steering group' and 'partnership forum'. In 2000, based on the success of the pilot programme, a team structure was developed across the entire plant accompanied by a 'gain-sharing' scheme. The benefits of partnership have been identified as the company getting significant organisational changes with employees having a significant say in these changes; a stable and flexible form of work organisation that is responsive to customer needs; changes in rewards systems including elimination of overtime, annualised hours and the 'gain-sharing' scheme; reduced time being spent on industrial relations issues; improved management-union relations and a better understanding by employees of customer needs and market demands.

The Incidence of Workplace Partnership

More than ten years on what can we say about the incidence of partnership in the workplace? To a large extent the answer depends on what meaning we choose to give to the term 'partnership'. We have already seen that the definition of partnership in *Partnership 2000* was broad enough to apply in both union and non-union settings and through formal and informal arrangements. Our interest is in management-union partnership arrangements. What evidence is there, then, of partnership arrangements of this type?

The research findings suggest strongly that the incidence of formal partnerships at workplace level is small. A comprehensive survey of organisations in the private and commercial state sectors, carried out before *Partnership 2000* was implemented, showed that of four approaches to organisational change available to managers (issues determined solely by management, issues decided through traditional collective bargaining with trade unions, issues decided by involving trade unions on a partnership basis, and issues decided by management with the direct involvement of employees) managers only used partnership to introduce change in about a fifth of workplaces (Roche et al., 1998). Managerial prerogative remained the most common approach to handling change in unionised workplaces. Partnership was rarely used in respect to changes in strategic areas such as the introduction of new products and services and, where it was used, it was mostly to address changes to working practices, payment systems, and working time arrangements (Roche et al., 1998). At most about 20 per cent of organisations had used partnership as an approach to change (Roche et al., 1998).

Since then, a 2003 survey of public and private sector employments showed that as few as 4 per cent of overall respondents had 'formal partnership agreements involving unions and employees' (NCPP, 2004). This figure increased to 15 per cent in the case of traditional manufacturing and to almost 30 per cent in the case of firms with 50 or more employees (NCPP, 2004). These findings appear to fit with the findings from the earlier UCD survey (Roche et al., 1998) and confirm that partnership is likely to be found in a minority of organisations but perhaps to a higher extent in large, manufacturing firms than in others.

There are at least two ways of interpreting these findings. One is to focus on the very low overall incidence of partnerships across all employments and to conclude that the various initiatives taken in support of partnership have not borne fruit to any significant degree. The other way is to focus on the higher incidence of partnership in large, unionised companies and to acknowledge that it is a significant development that 30 per cent of these organisations have formal management-union partnerships given the historically adversarial character of industrial relations in such firms. It can be stated with certainty that there has not been any widespread development of partnership since the late 1990s when it became the national policy of government and the social partners (Roche, 2006(a)). We will return to this issue in the final chapter.

Summary and Conclusions

In this chapter we saw that social partnership at national level provided the framework for employer and trade union agreement on the development of partnership at workplace level. As defined in *Partnership 2000*, partnership constituted a distinctive approach to organisational change in the unionised sector. Government, IBEC and ICTU committed themselves to a 'single guiding vision' for employment relations at workplace level. IBEC and ICTU invested considerable effort in separate and joint promotional activities aimed at encouraging adoption of partnership. Despite these and other initiatives since the late 1990s the evidence suggests that partnership is a minority practice in the unionised parts of the private sector.

3

FROM ADVERSARIALISM TO PARTNERSHIP

How can we explain why management and trade unions decide in certain organisations but not in others to shift from adversarialism to partnership as their preferred approach to day-to-day engagement and the handling of organisational change? How does partnership work in practice in terms of structures, agendas and processes? What outcomes does partnership produce for management, employees and trade unions? What challenges does partnership generate for the parties? Does it lead to the so-called 'win-win' or 'mutual gains' outcomes satisfactory to all stakeholders? In this chapter we discuss these questions through a review of the literature and research that have built up around workplace partnership.

Defining Partnership

From the 1980s onwards in the USA and Canada a number of different terms were used to describe new ways of involving employees and union representatives in workplace operations and workplace change. Common terms included 'QWL' or 'quality of working life programmes' (Kochan et al., 1986; Eaton et al., 1992), 'labour-management co-operation' (Cooke, 1990) and 'labour-management committees' (Kochan et al., 1986). Less common terms included 'continuous bargaining' (Clarke and Haiven, 1999) and 'joint governance' (Cutcher-Gershenfeld and Verma, 1994). More recently in the USA, Canada, Ireland and the UK, 'partnership' and 'workplace partnership' have become the common terms to describe inclusive approaches to employee and trade union involvement in organisational decision making.

At the same time it is accepted that there is a lack of precision as to what the term 'partnership' means (Knell, 1999). Nevertheless there are some defining features of management-union partnership that we can highlight (Cooke, 1990). Firstly, partnership arrangements are deliberately configured to be separate from collective bargaining both in terms of agendas addressed and the group processes used. Secondly, partnership involves structured mechanisms to facilitate input from union representatives and/or employees into management decisions. Thirdly, a key objective of partnership is to achieve benefits for managers, employees and trade unions, the 'mutual gains' agenda.

This broad conceptualisation of partnership allows considerable scope for variety between cases in terms of specific goals, structures, processes, agendas and so on. All we need for the present is a broad definition that allows us to separate partnership from exclusively direct forms of employee involvement and from related but distinct phenomena such as 'new forms of work organisation' or 'high involvement work practices'.

Advocates and Critics

Debates on workplace partnership are often polarised between 'advocates' and 'critics' (Kochan et al., 1986). Advocates derive their position from a belief that adversarial industrial relations are no longer viable in the context of modern competitive pressures and the changing preferences of employees and union members (Roche and Geary, 2006). The main advocates of partnership in the USA, Kochan and Osterman (1994), promote partnership as a means to achieve higher productivity, product quality and innovation at firm level, as a means to revitalise the trade union movement, and as a means to achieve improvements for workers and the overall economy and society. Advocates assume a 'mixed-motive' relationship in which employers and employees have both common and conflicting goals that are capable of resolution through a mix of adversarial and integrative bargaining approaches (Walton and McKersie, 1965: 4).

The main critics of partnership write from a 'militant' and often Marxist perspective (Kelly, 2004; Parker and Slaughter, 1997; Grattan, 1997; Allen, 2000). One critical characterisation of partnership is that it is 'a recent expression of an old and well-tried employers' strategy' that 'entails logic of class collaboration which ultimately leaves no room for independent and militant trade unionism' (Kelly, 1999). Critics assume that, while a degree of co-operation is essential at workplace level, the workplace is nevertheless the site of inherent conflict between management's desire to control workers, through coercion if necessary, and worker resistance to such efforts (Parker and Slaughter, 1997). Critics urge abstention, where possible, from partnerships and strong control where this is not possible. They favour trade union reliance on the power of worker mobilisation through adversarial collective bargaining over co-operation through partnership.

Not all commentary, however, falls into these two perspectives. Dobbins (2008) differentiates 'pragmatic contingency' which emphasises the pragmatism often at the core of the search for co-operative work relations from the approaches of advocates and critics. Contingency perspectives, he says, observe that the adoption and outcomes of partnership are contingent on multiple contextual conditions including economic pressures, technology, labour market and institutional factors, and different management and worker choices (Dobbins, 2008: 16-17). He distinguishes this perspective from that of Kochan and Osterman (1994) and others through its greater emphasis on power, authority and control relations in explaining the employment relationship.

Framework for Discussing the Theory of Workplace Partnership

In Figure 3.1 we summarise our overall method for organising our discussion of the theoretical treatment of workplace partnership. We assume that the dominant relationship between managers, employees and unions is of a low trust, 'arms-length', adversarial type, as outlined earlier.

Figure 3.1: Overview of Workplace Partnership

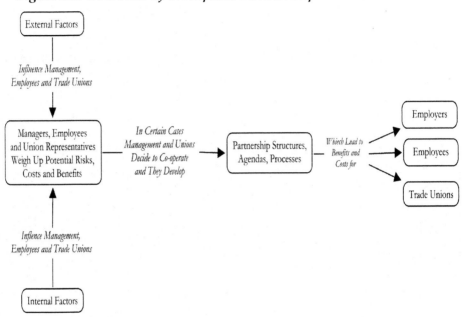

We assume that managers, employees and union representatives are influenced in their thinking and actions by deeply held attitudes and beliefs and by what they see happening in their organisations and in the wider economy and society. In some organisations the parties, having taken in and assessed various 'messages' from outside and inside the organisation, decide to co-operate through partnership. They establish structures and agree on agendas and on ways of working together. Partnership leads to outcomes in the form of benefits and costs to management, employees and trade unions. We will use this framework to organise our discussion of the literature on workplace partnership beginning with factors likely to influence decisions to adopt partnership.

Factors Influencing Decisions to Adopt Partnership

The Need for Change and the Risks of Change

Along with other writers on partnership, we borrow from the literature on organisational change the assumption that for change to happen there must first be some strong 'felt need' that change is necessary (Beckhard and Harris, 1977; Kochan and Dyer, 1976). This 'felt need' may arise from factors inside and/or outside the organisation. Developing partnership is itself a significant organisational change for managers and trade unions that carries economic and political risks. Risks for employers are that involving trade unions will either stymie change completely or slow it down considerably, that partnership will lead to a loss of managerial authority, to fear of loss of employment among middle managers and supervisors, to costly investment in training, and time wasted at meetings (Cooke, 1990; McKersie, 2002). Partnership may also impose constraints on flexibility through management commitments to pay and job security (Roche and Geary, 2006).

Risks for trade unions include workers seeing partnership as a substitute for collective bargaining and questioning the need for a union, unions being associated with unpopular decisions, and management getting benefits such as increased work effort with no tangible gains for members in return (Kochan et al., 1984; Wells, 1991; McKersie, 2002). For employers and trade unions there is the common risk of raising expectations that may not be met and of generating uncertainties around managerial decision-making and collective bargaining (HRDC, 1997 and 1998).

Management and trade unions have their own interests that inevitably come into sharp relief when they are weighing up the potential benefits and costs of partnership (HRDC, 1997). For em-

ployers, productivity increases and quality improvements are
likely to be important goals. For employees, job security, increased autonomy and improved working conditions are likely to
be important. For trade unions continued recognition and facilities, and influence over work organisation decisions are likely to
be important. As well as satisfying themselves that they can overcome the risks associated with partnership, the parties must also
judge that partnership will help them to achieve specific benefits
(Cooke, 1990). This is a complex matter because the parties do not
necessarily seek the same benefits, thus a benefit accruing to management from reduced costs may be perceived as a loss by employees and trade unions.

Theoretically, then, it appears that management and unions
will only seriously consider partnership if they feel intense pressure to do so, if they consider the likely benefits to outweigh the
likely costs, and if they perceive these benefits to be of greater
value than what they might achieve through traditional bargaining or through unilateral action (Kochan et al., 1984; Cooke, 1990).
What factors, then, does the research suggests might influence the
parties to develop partnership in the context of such potential
risks and potential benefits?

Economic and Relationships Crises

An economic crisis such as a threatened sale or closure of a plant
frequently provides the 'felt need' that encourages parties to consider partnership (Kochan and Osterman, 1994; Harrison and Laplante, 1996; HRDC, 1997). An economic crisis can generate enor-
mous pressure on employers to improve competitiveness and
productivity through internal organisational changes (Cooke,
1990; Kochan and Osterman, 1994; Walton et al., 1994). More intense competition and even the anticipation of more intense competition may also act as spurs to the consideration of partnership
(Roche and Geary, 2006). A relationships crisis such as a serious
industrial dispute or poor industrial relations over a long term

may provide the same effect (Cutcher-Gershenfeld and Verma, 1994; Kochan and Dyer, 1976). Some cases, however, grow in a planned manner through constructive engagement rather than through crisis, Shell Sarnia and Saturn Corporation for example (Heckscher, 1988; Rubinstein and Kochan, 2000).

The Quality of Management–Union–Employee Relationships

It seems that both high and low quality relationships may influence decisions to adopt partnership. Many cases in the USA (Cooke, 1990), Canada (Harrison and Laplante, 1996; Clarke and Haiven, 1999) and the UK (Marks et al., 1998; Lloyd and Newell, 2001) instance poor industrial relations, low levels of trust and industrial disputes as precipitating influences. While much of the discussion of low trust tends to focus on low employee trust in management, Guest and Peccei (2001: 231) conclude that management trust in employees is also generally low.

Sound relationships may also be an important influence on adoption of partnership, as we have already seen in the case of Shell Sarnia and Saturn Corporation. Kochan et al. (1984; 15) cite the Xerox Corporation in the USA where partnership was built on a bargaining relationship that was historically characterised by high levels of co-operation. A climate of co-operation and trust may be necessary for the development of partnership (Kochan and Osterman, 1994) and such a climate can be created where it does not currently exist through preparatory work aimed at relationship and trust building (Bushe, 1988; Cutcher-Gershenfeld and Verma, 1994; Totterdill and Sharpe, 1999: 34).

Business Strategies

The adoption of partnership has been associated with competitive strategies based on quality and innovation, the so-called 'high road' business strategies (Kochan and Osterman, 1994). Where companies compete solely or primarily through price competition it seems less likely that they will want to develop what they might perceive as costly or unnecessary innovations in management-union relationships and work organisation (Kochan and Osterman, 1994; Geary, 1999).

Manufacturing Industry and New Forms of Work Organisation

Most of the headline partnership cases have traditionally come from the manufacturing sector and initiatives in services such as banking and finance or the retail sector are less common (Kochan et al., 1984; Bushe, 1988; Kochan and Osterman, 1994; HRDC, 1997; Kelly, 2004). A recent US exception to this is the Kaiser Permanente partnership (Eaton et al., 2003; Kochan et al., 2008). Obvious Irish cases outside manufacturing are Allied Irish Banks (O'Dowd, 1998), Jury's Hotels (NCPP, 2002) and TESCO Ireland (IRN, 23 June 2005).

The introduction of new forms of work organisation as an approach to achieving higher productivity and increased competitiveness is often associated with partnership. There are a number of reasons why this might happen. Firstly, changes sought by employers generally include work organisation changes *and* industrial relations changes. Adversarial 'arms-length' relationships are considered antipathetic to the type of workplace relationships required for new work systems to be effective (ICTU, 1993: 16). Hence, in unionised employments a change in the quality of industrial relations is a prerequisite to the introduction of new forms of work organisation (HRDC, 1997). Secondly, securing willing employee involvement in different kinds of problem-solving groups and teams becomes an important objective for managers but this cannot be taken for granted against a background of low involvement and low trust (Kochan and Osterman, 1994; Regini, 1995). Thirdly, new forms of work organisation generally cannot be introduced without trade union agreement and worker support in unionised organisations (Cutcher-Gershenfeld and Verma, 1994: 549; HRDC, 1997).

Employer and Trade Union Power

Employers and trade unions frequently rely on the exercise of power, through unilateral decision-making and industrial action, to achieve their goals. It has been argued that employers are more likely than trade unions to pursue power-based strategies given that in many situations they have a realisable option – and in all cases the theoretical option – of operating without trade unions (Crouch, 1994: 33; Kumar et al., 1998). Employers are more likely to implement changes unilaterally where union bargaining power is weak (Kumar et al., 1998). Not surprisingly, then, the presence of trade unions that are powerful enough to prevent union avoidance tactics and pragmatic enough to take on joint responsibilities can influence the adoption of partnership (Cutcher-Gershenfeld and Verma, 1994: 549).

Union weakness is not, however, incompatible with the adoption of partnership. For example, employers may force and entice weak trade unions into partnership through threats of marginalisation and derecognition (Marks et al., 1998; Kelly, 2004; Marchington et al., 2001: 66). The degree of union strength or weakness may shape the partnership agenda in favour of the interests of one side (Lloyd and Newell, 2001; Kelly, 2004). Kelly (2004) argues that partnerships in which there is a roughly equal balance of power between management and unions are more likely to reflect union interests than what he terms 'employer-dominant' partnerships.

Nevertheless, it seems unlikely that employers would adopt a partnership with trade unions that had insufficient strength to prevent them from deciding matters unilaterally or from dealing directly with employees if this was their preferred approach. It also seems unlikely that trade unions would adopt partnership where they deemed it possible to achieve their objectives through the use of power alone.

Employer Values and Policies

Employer and trade union responses to external and internal pressures for change are likely to be influenced by how they interpret these pressures (Amis et al., 2002). Values influence how parties interpret such signals from the environment and how they respond to them (Goll, 1991). Not surprisingly, then, employer espousal of 'worker-oriented values' (Osterman, 1994: 186) can be an important influence on the adoption of partnership (Kochan et al., 1984; Kochan and Osterman, 1994; Cutcher-Gershenfeld and Verma, 1994; Guest and Peccei, 2001). Such values include a willingness to recognise and work with trade unions, guaranteeing employment security, good general treatment of employees etc.

There is also evidence that in many cases employers do not hold 'worker-oriented values' and are hostile to trade unions (Cooke, 1990; Bacon and Storey, 2000; Marchington et al., 2001). Furthermore, the adoption of workplace partnership implies a longer-term policy commitment by employers but the research suggests that they are likely to behave in a short-term, contradictory and opportunist way depending more on circumstances than on values or policy (Bacon and Storey, 2000: 423; Godard, 1997). It may be more likely that employers will adopt partnership on the basis of a practical acceptance that it will help them to achieve the potential gains of changes that require the co-operation of employees and trade unions (Regini, 1995: 109).

Trade Union Values and Policies

Trade union values may also dispose them positively towards workplace partnership. Many trade unions have adopted strategies of active involvement in employer-driven workplace change (Olney, 1996; Harrison and Laplante, 1996: 107; Perline, 1999). The rationale for such a policy is that the interests of trade unions need to extend beyond pay and conditions to include the critical decisions that affect workers' security and wages, such as company strategy, allocation of resources, the use of technology and so on (Lazes and Savage, 1997: 184). This policy assumes that it is possible for trade unions to work in partnership with employers while also building the union and addressing their members' needs for job security and better wages and conditions. It also implies a shift in union values towards accepting some responsibility for organisational perform-ance, willingness to facilitate direct employee involvement, reduc-ing reliance on adversarial bargaining, and accepting new forms of engagement such as joint problem solving.

However, trade union policies need to be considered in the context of other factors such as their assessment of the extent to which management might share decision-making with them (Eaton, 1988: 24-51), the degree of crisis facing an organisation (Cutcher-Gershenfeld and Verma, 1994), the quality of industrial relations (Harrison and Laplante, 1996) and the adequacy of the collective bargaining system (Rubin and Rubin, 2000).

Top Management and Trade Union Support

In keeping with the literature on organisational change, writers on partnership suggests that strong leadership and support by top executives and union leaders is an important influence on the adoption and development of partnership (Kochan and Dyer, 1976; Cohen-Rosenthal and Burton, 1987; Woodworth and Meek, 1995; HRDC, 1998). The argument is that senior and middle man-agers and trade union members will be motivated to support partnership to the extent that they see visible commitment from top management and trade union leaders.

There are undoubtedly cases where there was such top-level commitment from the beginning (Kochan et al., 1984: 22). But there are also instances of successful partnerships in which only tentative management and trade union commitment to talk and see what happened existed at the outset (Bushe, 1988: 144). Research also suggests that management commitment can be an outcome of partnership where managers becoming convinced to accept more union involvement because they see improvements arising from partnership (Clarke and Haiven, 1999).

The Collective Bargaining Relationship

Cooke (1990) and Rubin and Rubin (1997) link the decision to develop partnership to the effectiveness of the current system of collective bargaining in meeting the goals of employers, employees and trade unions. The argument here is that management and unions must be satisfied that their collective bargaining arrangements are capable of handling the industrial relations agenda effectively (otherwise the focus of trade unions would be on increasing the effectiveness of collective bargaining rather than seeking alternatives to it) but not as capable of successfully handling organisational change. Hence it may appear necessary to have some alternative means to collective bargaining through which the parties can handle organisational change and improvement together.

Human Resource Practices

Kochan and Osterman (1994: 46-55) suggest that partnership organisations will either have or will develop certain human resource practices, such as high standards of employee selection, broad task design and teamwork, employee involvement in problem solving, job security, investment in training and development etc. that are supportive of partnership and workplace innovations. Such practices may be present in the organisation before the development of partnership or they may be developed as part of such an approach. The evidence from case studies (Harrison and Laplante: 1996; Bacon and Storey: 2000; Marks et al., 1998) shows that such human resource practices can be developed through partnership as well as being present before it is developed.

The Role of Public Policy

We have already seen that management and trade union decisions at firm level are influenced by what is happening in the wider economy and society. Public policy is frequently cited, therefore, as an important influence on the development of workplace partnership. Instruments such as legislation, advocacy and financial and technical supports from public agencies, and the force of collective agreements can have a positive influence on the adoption of partnership (Marchington, 1992; Ichniowski et al., 1996; Harrison and Laplante, 1996; HRDC, 1997).

In Ireland the state, national employer and trade union bodies, industrial relations agencies, and European Union institutions have all sponsored the adoption of workplace partnership (O'Donnell and Teague, 2000; SIPTU, 2000; NCPP, 2002). The involvement of IBEC and ICTU was critical in convincing employers and trade unions to adopt partnership at enterprise level (Totterdill and Sharpe, 1999; Healy, 2000; SIPTU, 2000; Wall, 2004). In the late 1990s, IBEC, ICTU, SIPTU and the IPC brought a number of companies into partnership arrangements that were supported through projects funded by the EU's ADAPT Programme, as discussed earlier (O'Dowd, 2002).

How Partnership Works

Partnership Structures

Partnership, in our usage of the term, requires management and trade unions to establish new bodies, separate from collective bargaining structures, in order to facilitate co-operative engagement between them. Agreed structures, roles, agendas, objectives etc. are typically negotiated and documented in a formal agreement before partnership structures are established (O'Dowd, 1998). Partnership facilitates a wider involvement by individual employees as well as union representatives with a wider group of managers than would typically be involved in the collective bargaining process.

In general partnership involves 'parallel structures' that empower management, trade union representatives and employees to work together using ground rules such as consensus decision-making that do not apply within the day-to-day operating procedures of the organisation or within collective bargaining (Herrick, 1985; Rankin and Mansell, 1986; Bushe, 1988). Partnership ground rules effectively injunct managers, employees and union representatives to behave in more democratic ways than is permitted in the mainstream organisation where decision-making authority, outside of collective bargaining where decisions are taken jointly, rests squarely with management.

Herrick (1985: 967-8) outlines a number of common 'rules' for partnership bodies: collective bargaining issues are excluded, the power of final decision making is retained by management, participation is mandatory for management representatives and voluntary for union representatives, individual grievances are excluded, and guarantees are included as to how certain issues will be handled such as increases in organisational productivity or disputes. Such rules substitute for and facilitate the development of the trust that is frequently absent at the outset (Herrick; 1985: 968).

External or internal facilitators are used in many cases to facilitate discussion and constructive engagement (Bushe, 1988; Cohen Rosenthal and Burton, 1987). Facilitators can help the parties to define problems and to work towards their own solutions using a 'process consultation' approach (Kessler and Purcell, 1994; Schein, 1999). Joint problem solving, interest based bargaining, consensus decision-making, and conflict resolution are commonly used (Peterson and Tracy, 1992). In multi-union situations all of the unions sit with management at a 'single table' even where they negotiate separately through collective bargaining. It can be difficult initially for managers and union representatives to work in a collaborative manner against a background of adversarial engagement and low trust. Partnership requires new skills and joint training is strongly recommended (Cohen-Rosenthal and Burton, 1987: 176-188).

Partnership structures tend to be at least 'two-tiered' (Rankin and Mansell, 1986). The first tier takes the form of 'representative' bodies such as 'steering committees' with roughly equal numbers of management and union nominees (Kochan et al., 1984; Heckscher, 1998; Cooke, 1990: 68). These groups are typically located at plant or organisation or corporate levels and might be expected to address 'strategic' issues through the involvement of senior company executives and union leaders (McKersie, 2002: 106). These bodies also lead the development of partnership in the organisation. They act as 'trouble shooters' when difficulties arise.

These bodies frequently spawn a second tier of committees that widen employee involvement (Kochan et al., 1984: 17-20; Cohen-Rosenthal and Burton, 1987: 113-114). These committees are likely to be found at departmental or 'shop floor' or work unit levels and to address 'operational' issues through the involvement of middle managers, supervisors, employees and shop stewards. They may be representative or they may involve employees directly (Cooke, 1990). In unionised workplaces, employees are likely to participate in 'direct' structures only if they have been sanctioned by their trade unions (Gill and Krieger, 2000: 123).

Partnership Agendas

When management and unions are establishing a partnership they generally agree on the types of issues and/or on the specific issues that they want to address in the new arrangements. 'Industrial relations issues', i.e. issues currently being handled or traditionally handled through collective bargaining were generally excluded (Thacker and Fields, 1987: 99). This meant that issues of a pay and conditions type as well as 'hard' change issues, such as new technology and changes in work practices, were considered 'inappropriate' to partnership or, at least, to partnership in its early stages.

As a consequence, the design of many partnership initiatives assumes a 'stages' approach to agenda development whereby 'hard' or difficult issues only come on the agenda, if at all, after participants have learned to work together and have built trust through the joint handling of 'soft' or non-controversial issues. For example, the early US 'QWL' initiatives tended to concentrate on 'soft' projects around physical accommodation and workplace facilities (Kochan et al., 1986; Thacker and Fields, 1987). More substantial issues such as changes in work organisation and compensation systems tended to come on the agenda later in the process, if at all (Kochan et al., 1986; Thacker and Fields, 1987). In some exceptional cases, however, a severe economic crisis might drive unions and employers to the immediate handling of difficult problems without the support of a 'bedding in' phase (Kochan et al., 1986; Lazes and Savage, 1997).

The terms 'strategic' and 'operational' have been applied to partnership agendas. Strategic issues might include major issues such as industry restructuring, strategic alliances, the development of policies etc. and operational issues might include the development of new work practices, problems relating to production etc. (McKersie, 2002; Gunnigle, 1998).

We have already seen that trade union and employer strength can influence partnership agendas (Kelly, 2004). There is evidence of employers seeking to include or exclude terms and conditions of employment depending on their assessments of trade union strength and of how inclusion or exclusion might be to their benefit (Bacon and Storey, 2000: 419-424). Marchington (1992) finds that where trade union membership is high and where trade union members are a required component of partnership bodies, the agenda tends to focus on issues concerning working conditions, health and safety and pay restructuring. In organisations that have weaker union involvement the agenda tends to focus on performance and quality issues that might be of more interest to management than to unions or employees. Some unions fear that partnership bodies involving non-union members would decide issues that would normally be decided through management-union bargaining (Marks et al., 1998: 20).

In Ireland, partnerships have addressed issues such as the elimination of overtime, new planning systems, waste reduction initiatives, changes in work practices, team working and communications, improving the quality of working life, gain sharing, investment in new machinery, designing and introducing change etc. (Totterdill and Sharpe, 1999; SIPTU, 2000; NCPP, 2002). Examples of what appear to be more 'strategic' agendas include company ownership, development of business strategies such as strategic alliances, handling strategic changes, particularly in the commercial state sector (Gunnigle, 1998; Hastings, 2001; Roche and Geary, 2001; McKersie, 2002).

Partnership and Industrial Relations

We have already seen that in the negotiation of partnership agreements, management and trade unions commonly seek to ensure that partnership agendas and structures are kept separate from industrial relations arrangements. Both management and trade unions frequently want to 'have the best of both worlds', i.e. to preserve the benefits of collective bargaining arrangements while experimenting with new approaches to workplace change and relationships (Herrick, 1985: 966).

In Ireland it is commonly held that partnership groups should not deal with industrial relations issues at least during the formative stages and not before the process is robust enough to manage contentious problems (ICTU, 1997; IBEC, 1998; SIPTU, 1999). The initial separation of agendas appears to provide a degree of security to the parties to explore what can be achieved through partnership without putting existing arrangements at risk (Herrick, 1985; Rankin and Mansell, 1986; Bushe, 1988: 145; Roche, 2002: 16). The most common positioning of partnership is as a supplement to collective bargaining and not as a replacement for it (Marchington, 1992). It is common to have a ground rule that parties will not withdraw from partnership as a means of resolving industrial relations issues (Eaton et al., 2003).

Sustaining separation between partnership and collective bargaining is not, however, a straightforward matter (Kochan et al., 1984: 29). As partnership develops, the parties frequently agree to blur the separation between partnership and industrial relations agendas for the simple reason that many of the issues that parties want to address are industrial relations issues (Bushe; 1988: 145). In some cases partnership groups move gradually into collective bargaining issues and in other cases the parties carry traditional topics of negotiation straight into the partnership process (Kochan et al., 1984: 38).

Whether the institutional boundaries between partnership and industrial relations are sharply drawn or not, various 'spill-over' effects between partnership and industrial relations were found to occur (Strauss, 1998b: 132-3). The creation of a high trust and positive employment relations climate through partnership could render established collective bargaining channels less adversarial or more effective. As partnership arrangements assume growing importance, issues might be expected to 'migrate' from collective bargaining to partnership forums. This might be interpreted as a benign outcome of growing trust and confidence in partnership by stakeholders, but can also be interpreted in a different way. Kelly (2004: 205) has warned that while the migration of issues from collective bargaining to partnership forums might not necessarily signify a weakening of unions, it was far more likely to do so than the movement of issues from partnership to collective bargaining.

Rankin and Mansell (1986) argue that separation of partner-ship from collective bargaining is a convenient fiction and that the overlap between them is an inevitable outcome of a mature change process. They argue that organisational improvement will be limited as long as issues covered by collective agreements are out of bounds because such issues have a direct bearing on organ-isational performance. As a consequence it is necessary to allow work organisation, collective bargaining and partnership to be-come 'integrated' rather than remain 'parallel' (Rankin and Mansell, 1986). In Ireland there has been an increased emphasis in recent years on 'mainstreaming' which appears to suggest moving away from a parallel structures approach (Roche, 2002; O'Donnell and Teague, 2000; NCPP, 2007).

Partnership and Management Decision Making

The degree of decision-making authority ceded to partnership bodies by employers can vary hugely and can be a source of ten-sion between management and trade unions. Partnership, by definition, implies some redistribution of power. The sharing of power and influence by employers, however, seems to run counter to the traditions of most organisations (McKersie, 2002: 113), a fact that has not been lost on employees (Freeman and Rogers, 1999).

In Ireland, SIPTU guidelines state that partnership should not inhibit the day-to-day management of the company. At the same time the union argues that it is important that management would cede a degree of decision-making authority to partnership groups (SIPTU, 1999; SIPTU, 2000). Partnership can also involve the ced-ing of authority by trade unions on industrial relations matters to partnership bodies or the ceding of the right of 'veto' over work-place change by shop stewards in return for influence at higher levels of decision-making.

There is evidence that companies involve unions in implemen-tation after management have made decisions unilaterally (Harrison and Laplante, 1996: 104-105). Partnership may give trade unions the opportunity to influence policies and procedures but the final decision-making authority, as we have seen, generally rests with management (Herrick, 1985; Marchington, 1992). The degree of involvement of unions in management decision-making can change over time. The trade union role may be defined in quite limited terms and then expand over time (Bushe, 1988: 145-146). In some cases joint decision making around specific issues may be agreed from the outset. Cutcher-Gershenfeld and Verma (1994) cite cases of 'joint governance' that provide for consensual decision making on specific issues. In Shell Sarnia and the Saturn Corporation (Heckscher, 1988; Rubinstein and Kochan, 2001) management and trade unions agreed from the outset that they would make important decisions jointly. There may be natural limitations on power sharing due to legislation and to company ownership (Clarke and Haiven, 1999:171).

Sustaining Partnership

Sustaining partnership over time and embedding it as day-to-day practice is a major challenge for employers and trade unions (Kochan and Dyer, 1976: 69; Kochan et al., 1984: 11). A number of major difficulties may arise. The external conditions that stimulated the decision to adopt partnership may change to such an extent as to significantly weaken the pressure on the parties to remain engaged. Or changed conditions may make it difficult for the parties to continue to attain valued goals (Kochan and Dyer, 1976). Management may be willing to co-operate with unions when economic conditions are bad but then lose interest when circumstances improve (HRDC, 1998). The survival rates of employee involvement initiatives can be very low with an attrition rate of up to two thirds after six years (Kochan and Osterman, 1994: 98-101). Cooke, however, found that only 11 per cent of partnership programmes had been terminated after six years (Cooke, 1990: 63).

Internal conditions may also change in ways that undermine partnership. For example, changes among senior management may lead to cost-minimisation strategies that undermine partnership such as opening non-union plants (Kochan and Osterman, 1994: 59-69). Changes in the relative strengths of the parties may also be a factor. It can be extremely difficult for employers and trade unions to resist the use of power when they become convinced that they can achieve more through power than through partnership (Hammer and Stern, 1986: 337-338; Cooke, 1990: 40). Rankin and Mansell (1986) argue that the very nature of 'parallel' partnership structures makes them easy to dismantle and that it suits management and unions to keep them 'parallel' where they do not want to change adversarial relationships in the long term.

Sustaining partnership is also problematical in terms of intergroup and intra-group dynamics. For example, there is inevitably going to be a degree of internal opposition (Kochan et al., 1984: 11). Usually, the groups that are most reticent to embrace partnership are middle management and highly skilled employees such as craft workers who tend to have strong bargaining power (Fenton-O'Creevy, 1998: 68; McKersie, 2002: 113; Kochan et al., 1984: 47; Clarke and Haiven, 1999: 175; Harrison et al., 2001).

Opposition from middle managers is often attributed to fear of losing power and to the fact that senior managers may espouse partnership but exclude middle managers from decision-making (Kochan et al., 1984: 24). Craft workers may fear the loss of privileged status in terms of work and of conditions of employment. In Ireland, however, there is evidence of craft trade unions embracing partnership in several companies including Waterford Glass, Aughinish Alumina (Dobbins, 2008), Air Atlanta (IRN, 26 July 2007), and Bausch and Lomb (IRN, 9 September 2004).

The voluntary character of partnership may also lead to inherent instability. Streeck (1992) argues that there is an inherent imbalance in power between employers and trade unions and that partnership is, by definition, focused around employers' market and productivity concerns and not those of trade unions. Unions must maintain 'good behaviour' to retain influence rather than enjoy influence as a right as they would in statutory systems.

Outcomes for Employers, Employees and Trade Unions

Outcomes for Employers

There is considerable evidence of positive outcomes for employers from 'high performance work systems', employee participation generally, and advanced human resource practices etc. (Roche and Geary, 2006; NCPP, 2003 and 2008). Relatively little research, however, has specifically focussed on the voluntary management-union partnerships that we are concerned with in this book.

In his study of partnership in US manufacturing firms, Cooke (1990) distinguishes between improvements in company performance that are brought about directly through improved productivity, product quality, and efficiency and indirectly through improved relationships between managers, supervisors, employees and union representatives. Many studies, particularly from the USA and Canada, identify direct organisational performance outcomes such as reduced absenteeism; fewer accidents, fewer grievances, and quits (Havlovic, 1991; Clarke and Haiven, 1999); improved product and service quality (Voos, 1987; Cooke, 1990; Rubinstein, 2000); improvements in productivity, labour cost per unit of output, and profit per unit of sales (Voos, 1987; Marks et al., 1998; Black and Lynch, 1997 and 2000); quality and innovation, sales, customers and profits (Guest and Peccei:2001: 227-230). Not all studies, however, report substantial positive outcomes. For example, some US studies only report limited economic and industrial relations performance improvements (Katz et al., 1983; Schuster, 1983). Nevertheless, there is strong evidence that partnership can lead to positive outcomes for employers.

Outcomes for Employees

The major gain for employees from partnership is enhanced security of employment (Harrison and Laplante, 1996; Marks et al., 1998; Clarke and Haiven, 1999). Other benefits include more information and better communications from management (Marchington, 1992); higher investment in training and development and improved rewards packages (Marks et al., 1998; HRDC, 1998; Clarke and Haiven, 1999); increased job satisfaction and strong identification with the organisation's objectives and values (Batt and Applebaum, 1995; Knell, 1999); improved quality of working life (HRDC, 1998) and some degree of influence over workplace issues (Kochan et al., 1984). There is strong evidence that employees want to have a say in decisions affecting their jobs and work environment and that they react positively to participation (Kochan and Osterman, 1994: 70-71; Freeman and Rogers, 1999).

Not all research, however, paints such a positive picture for employees. Kelly (2004) concludes that along measures of employment security, job losses and wage movements, partnership has at best produced mixed outcomes and probably has produced few gains for employees. There is also evidence that partnership may lead to increased employee expectations and to frustration, tension and cynicism if such expectations are not met (HRDC, 1998).

There is mixed evidence as to the effects of the high performance work systems frequently associated with partnership. Some evidence points to high levels of worker satisfaction with management-union relations (Freeman and Rogers, 1999) but other evidence suggests that such practices may lead to insecure, stressful working environments and that new work systems can lead to a loss of control and autonomy and to increased demands on workers (Kumar, 2000). A study of partnership initiatives in two UK aerospace companies suggests that employers benefited from cost reductions and increased productivity while employees experienced increased job insecurity, work intensification and reduced job autonomy (Danford et al., 2005). A study of partnership in a UK insurance company where a union is recognised suggests that employees generally felt that they were being informed about decisions rather than being involved (Tailby et al., 2005: 218-9).

Outcomes for Trade Unions

Overall, advocates of partnership assert that unions can only survive and serve their members by embracing and shaping partnership while critics argue that adversarial relationships serve trade unions well and that partnership is a recipe for marginalisation (Peetz, 1996). Studies suggest that when unions act as joint sponsors of partnership, there will generally be positive outcomes in terms of institutional security (Marks et al., 1998) and membership commitment to and involvement in the union (Kochan et al., 1984; Verma, 1989; Eaton et al., 1992; Freeman et al., 2000). Union activists and officials as well as rank-and-file members generally have a very positive attitude towards worker participation programmes (Kochan et al., 1984).

There is also evidence that union members consider their union to have a higher level of influence in job areas where they were not traditionally involved such as implementing technological changes as a result of union involvement in partnership (Thacker and Fields, 1987; Clarke and Haiven, 1999). The evidence also suggests that the bargaining power of unions in traditional areas of pay and conditions is strengthened by the union becoming involved in work organisation and business planning and decision-making (Kaminski, 1997; Clarke and Haiven, 1999; Rubinstein and Kochan, 2001).

Research in the financial services sector in Australia suggests that a cooperative labour relations climate was associated with improvements in organisational productivity as well as increased loyalty to the union among its members (Deery and Iverson, 2005). There is some evidence that union members appear to want their unions to play both co-operative and adversarial roles at once, the former on issues not covered by collective bargaining such as work organisation and the latter on pay and conditions (Eaton et al., 1992; Geary, 2006).

Not all researchers support such a positive picture for trade unions. There is evidence that non-involvement by unions (Verma and McKersie, 1987) can be a threat in that union members who then become involved in partnership activities may be less active in the union and employee identification with the company and its goals may increase without a similar benefit to the union. Partnership may confer new roles on full-time officials such as involvement with managers at strategic levels but at the same time pose threats to the authority and role of shop-floor representatives as the 'voice' of the workers. This can happen where partnership involves direct worker involvement in decision-making about workplace change (Marks et al., 1998; Marchington et al., 2001: 64). Or the achievement of strategic influence by trade unions may involve a trade-off involving concessions on conditions of employment (Gilson and Wagar, 2000). Kelly concludes from a review of UK cases that whilst senior union representatives have sometimes become more involved in corporate decision-making, reliable evidence on actual influence is patchy (Kelly, 2004: 12). A study of partnership in a UK insurance company where a union is recognised suggests that unions had little influence through the representative arrangements (Tailby et al., 2007: 226).

In some cases partnership was seen to have divided unions, leading to both intra-union and inter-union conflict. The participation of union members in various forms of direct involvement and the admission of unions to representative structures disguised management dominance of agenda setting and priorities (Danford et al., 2005). Partnership served to incorporate unions into a management-dominated agenda, to their own disadvantage and that of their members (Danford et al., 2005).

Critics conclude that although providing some formal insurance for union recognition, partnership facilitates corporate downsizing, weakens traditional union prerogatives, fails to increase union influence and results in a decline in the strength of the local trade union (Taylor and Ramsay, 1998; Rosen, 1998; Kelly, 1999 and 2004). Peetz (1996), however, argues that outcomes of partnership such as incorporation are conditional on trade union behaviour and that if trade unions are doing their job, in the eyes of members, management efforts to develop more inclusive work relationships will do no harm to unionisation and may actually enhance it.

Critics, in most cases, do not consider the dynamics of partnership in depth, for example, how trade union characteristics and behaviour might interact with employer behaviour to influence outcomes except in so far as they acknowledge that strong unions are more likely to influence content and outcomes than weak unions (Kelly, 2004). But there is evidence that union capabilities including the abilities to access information, to educate and mobilise members, to access decision-making at multiple points in the organisation, and to balance co-operation and conflict are significant as far as outcomes for unions are concerned (Frost, 2000).

We have some insights into the challenges that partnership can generate for trade unions in a study of interest-based negotiation within the Kaiser Permanente Partnership in the USA (Eaton et al, 2008). The key challenges identified for trade unions are: ensuring an appropriate balance in terms of time and resources between partnership and collective bargaining; developing new skills in business areas as well as in areas such as problem solving, planning and consensus building; balancing the demands of partnership with the need to organise and increase membership; balancing power-based and co-operation-based activities in engaging with management; and, in the case of multi-union partnerships, managing inter-union relations.

Outcomes for Employers, Employees and Trade Unions

Partnership can have positive outcomes for management-union-employee relationships generally and for collective bargaining in particular. Partnership can lead to improved relationships, increased trust, a better atmosphere at work, information sharing, more dialogue, less adversarialism, agreement on issues that are too complex to be handled effectively by collective bargaining, more positive attitudes towards change in general, and the identification of areas of joint concern, employee loyalty and trust towards the firm, and employee morale (Heckscher, 1988: 150; HRDC, 1998; Marks et al., 1998; Marchington, 1992; Clarke and Haiven, 1999; Batt and Applebaum, 1995; Freeman and Rogers, 1999:107-109).

These 'relationships' outcomes are likely to have an indirect impact on organisational performance. For example, improved communications and higher levels of trust can lead to improved relationships which in turn can help management and trade unions jointly address problems associated with productivity and quality that have 'bottom line' implications (Cooke, 1990). Partnership can also have positive impacts on collective bargaining by facilitating negotiations and reducing the time required to reach agreement (HRDC, 1998).

In sum, then, it appears that partnership can deliver positive outcomes for management, employees and trade unions and in that sense it can deliver 'mutual gains'. What is less clear is whether any one party gains more than others.

Explaining Outcomes

It has been argued that the key question about employee participation is not so much whether it 'works' but rather under what conditions it will best function. In seeking to explain how partnership leads to significant positive outcomes for the parties, researchers have tended to focus in the main on partnership structures and partnership agendas. Of these two dimensions, re-searchers have tended to focus more on the influence of structures than agendas.

Partnership Structures and Outcomes

We can find three approaches to explaining how partnership structures influence significant outcomes (O'Dowd and Roche, 2009). The first approach assumes that direct and representative forms of partnership can have equal effects on outcomes. In his study of 'committee-based' or representative partnership ar-rangements and 'team-based' or direct partnership arrangements in unionised US manufacturing plants, Cooke (1990: 63-4) found that both types of arrangements had equivalent effects on a num-ber of company performance outcomes, provided that partnership activity in each case was of high 'intensity' (Cooke, 1990: ch. 4). Cooke defined 'high intensity' in terms of high workforce cover-age, frequent meetings, well-structured agendas, training in the conduct of joint activity and the involvement of union officials and plant management (Cooke, 1990: 95). This approach, how-ever, precluded consideration of whether initiatives that involved both direct and representative forms of partnership together might have different and even superior outcomes to initiatives that involved mainly direct or representative forms only.

A second approach to explaining how partnership structures influence outcomes assumes that 'more is better than less' when it comes to employee involvement arrangements and that multi-level arrangements involving both direct and representative forms of involvement at strategic and operational levels of organisation are better than arrangements at any one level or of any one type. An example of this approach is Kochan and Osterman's classic model of the 'mutual gains enterprise', in which participation in strategic decision-making through representative structures of various kinds and various direct forms of involvement are identi-fied as key components of partnership (Kochan and Osterman,

1994: 55-8, 47-52). Other examples of this approach to how partnership structures influence outcomes are found in Guest and Peccei's (2001) study of partnership companies and in a study of partnership in two NHS trusts in Northern Ireland (Heaton et al., 2002).

A third approach to explaining how partnership structures influence outcomes assumes that strategic or representative and direct or operational forms of partnership are 'functionally interdependent' in the sense that the effectiveness of either form is dependent on the presence of the other form. The work of Cutcher-Gershenfeld and Verma (1994) provides a striking example of this approach. For Cutcher-Gershenfeld and Verma direct forms of involvement, such as teamwork, project and problem-solving groups, are important ways of addressing operational improvements in work practices that can deliver improved company performance and that can leverage the effort of sizeable sections of the workforce (Cutcher-Gershenfeld and Verma, 1994: 566-7). The same can be argued with respect to other operational-level partnership initiatives, such as continuous/process improvement teams, joint working parties, partnership forums etc. that might involve employees on a representative as well as on a direct basis.

However, when undertaken in isolation, direct or other operational-level initiatives can be problematical. For example, they may lack legitimacy in the eyes of employees and managers. In unionised workplaces, for example, employees are likely to participate in such initiatives only if participation is sanctioned by their trade unions and if these initiatives are monitored by unions involved in representative partnership arrangements at a more strategic level (Gill and Krieger, 2000: 123). In the case of management, it has been argued that unless representative arrangements exist at a 'higher level' within organisations, managers and supervisors, focused on their own interests and possibly hostile to participation, may block or distort the expression of employee interests and views to senior management (Strauss, 1998a: 26-7).

Evidence from Ireland suggests that middle managers and supervisors are also more likely to be actively engaged in partnership where it is legitimised through the involvement of higher-level managers (Roche and Geary, 2006).

A second problem where direct or operational-level involvement alone is adopted is that through these forms of involvement organisational changes might be identified that are only capable of being addressed at a more strategic level through representative partnerships. Without the facility of having such changes addressed at a higher level, involvement focused on operational issues might lead to tensions and frustrations between management, employees and union members (Cutcher-Gershenfeld and Verma, 1994: 566-7).

Representative partnership arrangements, particularly at the strategic level, are likely to involve senior managers and senior full-time trade union officials who are capable of dealing with significant change agendas and of generating support for partnership among managers, employees and representatives working together at operational level. Strategic partnership arrangements may also integrate partnership activities with strategic decision-making, thus providing focus and cohesion for partnership (Strauss, 1998a: 26-7; Kochan and Osterman, 1994: 55-8).

However, when undertaken in isolation, representative partnership arrangements, particularly at the strategic level can also be problematical. For example, such forms may involve too few personnel to influence directly the kinds of changes at an operational level that can improve the performance of companies and the conditions of employees (Cutcher-Gershenfeld and Verma, 1994: 564-7).

In other words, the effectiveness of representative partnership arrangements may be dependent on the existence of direct or operational-level initiatives just as the effectiveness of operational partnership arrangements may be dependent on the existence of strategic partnership arrangements. It appears essential, therefore, to have mutually reinforcing linkages between these two types or levels of partnership structures in order to achieve significant positive outcomes. Guest and Peccei (2001: 228-32) found that direct involvement combined with representative involvement in organisational decisions was found to have positive outcomes for employees and employers. In Ireland, Dobbins (2008) also found that the effectiveness of joint management-union initiatives in Waterford Glass and Aughinish Alumina were influenced by the extent to which they combined representative and direct forms of involvement. The Aer Rianta case also highlighted the value of having partnership at both operational and strategic levels (Roche and Geary, 2006).

Partnership Agendas and Outcomes

We have already seen that the early literature on co-operative employment relations commonly distinguished between issues suited to partnership and issues more amenable to traditional collective bargaining (Cooke, 1990; Herrick, 1985; Woodward and Meek, 1994). In effect, this meant that many issues – quintessentially, pay and conditions but also other 'hard' issues such as new technology or changes in work practices – were considered inappropriate for partnership, at least in its early stages. Researchers found, however, that early US initiatives in improving QWL, whatever their effects on workplace relationships and the quality of work life, failed to produce measurable and sustained improvements in productivity and quality. This was because such performance outcomes were dependant not alone on breaking down traditional adversarial relationships, but also on changes in work organisation and design (Kochan et al., 1986; Kochan and Osterman, 1994: 66-7).

Reflecting these findings the early injunction to avoid dealing with 'hard' industrial relations issues in partnership arrangements became problematic or was significantly diluted. A number of post-1990 case studies of partnership in the US, Canada, the UK and Ireland pointed to partnership agendas that focused on a diverse mix of issues, like change and restructuring, product quality, productivity, commercial strategy and business challenges, industrial relations reform, shop-floor relationships and communications, work organisation, flexibility, team working, new organisational structures and changes in pay arrangements and conditions of employment (Roche and Geary, 2006; Rubinstein and Kochan, 2001; Knell, 1999; Harrison and Laplante, 1996; Cutcher-Gershenfeld and Verma, 1994). It appeared, therefore, that partnership agendas had sometimes become broader in scope and more focused on 'mainstream' issues of central concern for employers, employees and trade unions, and that the institutional separation of partnership and industrial relations agendas and structures had sometimes become greatly diluted in practice.

Today, in many instances in Ireland there is probably less emphasis on keeping the industrial relations agenda separate from the partnership agenda other than in the early stages of development when processes and relationships might not be deemed robust enough for handling such issues. An important implication of the 'mainstream' idea is that no issue, including issues that might be considered to be of an industrial relations type, is inappropriate to partnership provided that the parties voluntarily agree to it being on the agenda.

What, then, can be said about 'mainstream' agendas in practice? In terms of specific agenda items, the NCPP instances the principles and practices identified by Guest and Peccei (2001) as 'key components' of partnership (NCPP, 2003: 14). Translated into agenda items this gives a wide-ranging agenda encompassing production issues, pay and conditions of employment, personal employment decisions, employee related issues such as staffing levels, organisational issues such as major capital investment, flexible job design and focus on quality, performance management, employee share ownership, workplace communications, conditions of employment such as pension schemes, and employment security (NCPP, 2003: 14).

The NCPP cite cases including Tegral Metal Forming, Dairygold and Jury's Hotels that between them had agendas encompassing work re-organisation, introduction of new technology, new work practices/organisation structures, new pay systems, cost savings, pensions, business process improvements, skills development, dissemination of business information, harmonisation of work conditions, and cost savings (NCPP, 2002:12-14). The early EU-funded projects also had agendas that mixed quality of working life and business issues (Totterdill and Sharpe, 1999; SIPTU, 2000; NCPP, 2002).

Given the different circumstances and problems facing different organisations it does not seem reasonable to expect that certain 'generic' items should appear on all partnership agendas, although it has to be noted that the NCPP cases do have certain similarities as far as agendas are concerned. Nevertheless, it does seem that significant performance outcomes are more likely to be achieved where there is a broad or 'mainstream' agenda than where the agenda is largely focused on employee concerns such as the quality of working life. A 'mainstream' agenda involves a mix of agenda items relating to industrial relations issues and structures, workplace relationships between managers/super-visors and employees, and business issues relating to work organisation, job design, work practices etc. It also includes 'soft' issues such as job sharing, skills development, and communications.

In sum, then, it appears that for partnership arrangements to be capable of delivering significant outcomes to the parties, that they need to encompass both strategic and representative structures as well as operational or direct involvement structures, and also to encompass a 'mainstream' agenda comprising 'hard' business issues and 'soft' relationships issues.

6¿

Conclusions

.pter we have seen that the adoption and operations of .ship are influenced by a complex interplay of external and .rnal factors. For example, pressures to adopt partnership may come from external competitive threats but internal factors such as the quality of industrial relations also need to be taken into account. Most partnership bodies appear to operate 'in parallel' to pre-existing organisational structures and processes. Major boundary management problems arise for employers and trade unions regarding collective bargaining and management decision-making. Sustaining partnership is also problematical.

On the balance of the evidence available, partnership appears to be associated with more positive than negative outcomes for employers, employees and trade unions. An important issue is the extent to which parties benefit relative to each other – the 'mutual gains' scenario. However, explaining *how* partnership produces the effects that it does is far from straightforward. The most convincing explanations for successful outcomes hinge around the agendas that the parties select for partnership and the structures that are developed to address these agendas. We will examine these issues again the context of the survey findings that we will report in the next four chapters.

4

INFLUENCES ON THE ADOPTION
OF PARTNERSHIP

We saw in the last chapter that organisations adopted partner-ship as a result of a multiplicity of external and internal in-fluences. In this chapter we outline and discuss the reasons why the companies that took part in our survey decided to develop their partnerships. We begin with a description of these companies in terms of size, sector, age and ownership. We also report findings on management-union relations, trade union membership and other internal features. We look at human resource practices in these or-ganisations before partnership was introduced. We then go on to discuss the reasons why they developed partnership.

Overview of Organisations

Dates of Establishment

The vast majority (79.3 per cent) of the 88 cases that we included in our analysis were established between 1997 and 2000 with the remaining 20.7 per cent being established between 1987 and 1996, as indicated in Table 4.1. Ten respondents did not give dates of establishment.

The low incidence of cases pre-1987 may be explained by the weak tradition prior to the late 1990s of employee and trade union involvement in workplace change outside of collective bargaining (Kelly and Hourihan, 1994).

Table 4.1: Dates of Establishment of Partnership

Year	Number of Cases	% of Cases
1987-1995	10	13.0
1996	6	7.7
1997	15	19.2
1998	27	34.6
1999	14	17.9
2000	6	7.7
Total	78	100

It is worth noting again that the first national programme to actively promote workplace partnership, *Partnership 2000* (Government of Ireland, 1997) was signed in 1997. The preceding programme, the *Programme for Competitiveness and Work* (Government of Ireland, 1994) facilitated private sector bargaining at enterprise level around pay and change, as we saw earlier, and certain of the local deals struck had provisions for the development of partnership structures and activities. We also saw that SIPTU in particular made a point of seeking the establishment of partnership forums as part of their local bargaining strategy (IRN, 29 October 1998). It appears, then, that many of the cases established in the years 1997 and 1998 might have arisen in part from the negotiation of local pay and change agreements.

We have seen that in the USA it was employers in the main that took the initiative in developing workplace partnership (Cooke, 1990). We saw that this was also the case in Ireland with works committees in the 1970s. However, the impetus for the partnership initiatives of the late 1990s was shared to a far greater extent between employers and trade unions. More than a third (37.2 per cent) of respondents said that employers took the initiative, 8.1 per cent said trade unions took the initiative and more than half (54.7 per cent) said partnership was a joint initiative.

Partnership can be 'informal' in the sense that it can emerge as a set of values and practices without these being codified or formalised (NCPP, 2002). Trade unions, however, tend to seek formal agreements around the establishment of partnership (ICTU, 1997; SIPTU, 1999). More than half (59.1 per cent) of all respondents said that there was a formal partnership agreement in place. In sum, it seems reasonable to conclude that these partnerships arose as innovations within existing industrial relations systems rather than being initiated or sponsored from other sources within the organisations concerned.

Economic Sector

Most respondents were private sector manufacturing firms (55.7 per cent), which is not surprising given the strong associations between partnership, new forms of work organisation and manufacturing industry in other countries (Kochan et al., 1984; Bushe, 1988; Kochan and Osterman, 1994; HRDC, 1997; Kelly, 2004). Also, we have seen that many of the respondents had taken part in various EU-funded programmes that were aimed in the main at manufacturing firms.

Respondents from the services sector, including commercial state companies, amounted to more than a quarter of the respondents (28.4 per cent). Given the exclusion from the survey of centrally agreed partnership initiatives in the civil service, local authorities, the health and education sectors etc. it is not surprising that a small portion of the respondents (10.2 per cent) were from these core public services. It will be recalled that the cases included were ones where management and trade unions had decided at local level to develop some form of joint working, sometimes called 'partnership' and sometimes not, in advance of the national adoption by public service employers and trade unions of *Partnership 2000*.

A slight majority of the respondents were foreign-owned companies (54.5 per cent). Foreign ownership was spread as follows among the 43 companies that gave details (out of 48): USA (18), Germany (7), UK (4), Japan (3), Belgium (2), Switzerland (2), France (2), and one each from Sweden, Denmark, Holland, Finland, and Northern Ireland. More than a quarter (26.1 per cent) were partly or wholly Irish-owned private companies and almost one in five were Irish state-owned (19.3 per cent). It will be re-called that several Irish state-owned companies were obliged by law to have specific forms of employee involvement at board and sub-board levels (Kelly and Hourihan, 1994).

Organisation Size and Age

The total number of employees in the 87 organisations that gave details of employment size was 126,230 or 9.5 per cent of the total number of employees at work in 2000. Figure 4.1 indicates that as few as 12.5 per cent of respondents had between 20 and 99 em-ployees. A little less than a quarter (21.6 per cent) had between 100 and 249 employees. At the upper end of the size scale, 22.7 per cent had between 250 and 499 employees and 43.2 per cent had 500 plus employees.

Figure 4.1: Organisation Size

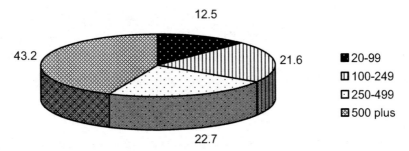

Thus, with almost seven out of ten organisations (65.9 per cent) having more than 250 employees, workplace partnership appears to be related to the size of organisations. The findings on manufacturing sector and on organisation size appear to fit with the findings of the 2004 NCPP survey which indicated that organisations in traditional manufacturing and with 50 or more employees were more likely to have formal partnership arrangements involving trade unions than others (NCPP, 2004). These findings appear similar to the experience in the UK (Cully et al., 1999). The incidence of partnership in large organisations is not surprising given that the greatest concentration of trade union membership in the private sector is in large organisations (Geary, 2006) and that such organisations tend to have more formalised employee relations systems than smaller ones. In Chapter One we saw that works committees were more likely to be found in large than in small manufacturing firms.

Almost nine out of ten respondents (88.6 per cent) said they had formal grievance and disciplinary procedures. This compares with 69.5 per cent in the case of 'formal dispute resolution procedures' in union and non-union firms with 50 or more employees (NCPP, 2003).

There was a considerable degree of variation between respondents in terms of organisation age, see Figure 4.2.

Figure 4.2: Organisation Age

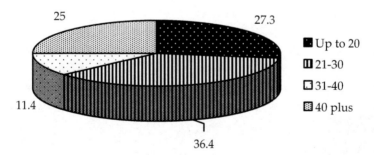

Slightly more than a quarter of respondents (27.3 per cent) were up to twenty years old. More than a third (36.4 per cent) were in operation for between 21 and 30 years and 11.4 per cent were in operation for 31 to 40 years. A further quarter (25 per cent) was in operation for more than 40 years. Almost three quarters of the organisations (72.8 per cent) were in operation for 21 years or more. Only 6.8 per cent were 10 years or less in operation.

The trend, then, among respondents was towards larger and older organisations. This is not surprising given that many younger and smaller companies, especially US multinationals, are non-union and fall outside the scope of the research and also that unionised organisations are more likely to be large and mature rather than young and small. It is also likely that long-established, unionised organisations would have deeply embedded adversarial industrial relations cultures that might constitute a significant barrier to the introduction of organisational changes that needed employee and trade union co-operation.

External Influences on Adoption of Partnership

Reasons for Adopting Partnership

We show the responses from the 80 companies in the private and commercial state sectors in Figure 4.3. We see that the most important reason for adopting partnership at 60.7 per cent was the anticipation of significant future changes in respondents' commercial situation for which they wanted to prepare the organisation.

Figure 4.3: Principal Reasons for Adopting Partnership

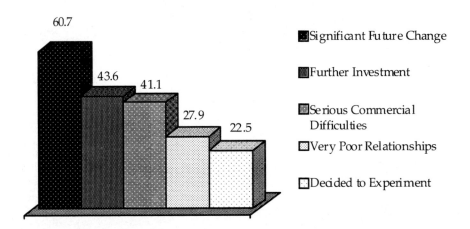

Second in importance at 43.6 per cent was the need for further investment, which could only be obtained on the basis of major changes in management-union relations and working practices. Third in importance at 41.1 per cent was serious commercial difficulties necessitating significant changes for which the support of the workforce was required. Fourth in importance at 27.9 per cent was a very poor relationship with the workforce and trade unions. Least of the five in importance at 22.5 per cent was experimenting with partnership to see how it worked and what benefits it might bring.

These findings are interesting on a number of counts. The fact that anticipation of future changes was the most important reason for adopting partnership suggests more of a planned than a crisis-driven approach to change in these organisations. This is supported by the emergence of the need for further investment as the second most commonly cited important reason. The finding that serious commercial difficulties and very poor relationships only ranked third and fourth, respectively, in order of importance is consistent with the findings on anticipation of future changes and the need for further investment. However, it appears to run counter to the findings in the international literature that it takes an economic or relationships crisis in most instances to spur the adoption of partnership in the workplace (Kochan and Dyer, 1976; Kochan and Osterman, 1994; Cutcher-Gershenfeld and Verma, 1994). In the UK, recent research found that 'adaptation', defined as gradually modernising working practices and industrial relations to new emerging market requirements, was the main employer aim in 64 per cent of recent partnership agreements (Bacon, 2007).

It is not surprising that last in importance is experimentation given that partnership carries strong risks for employers and trade unions (Kochan et al., 1984; McKersie, 2002; Cooke, 1990) and, consequently, it can be inferred that they would be unlikely to take such risks simply on the basis of experimentation.

One explanation for this apparent 'planned' as opposed to cri-sis-driven approach could be that the wider context in which these partnerships were developed involved government and the social partners encouraging a planned approach to organisational change through national agreements and the EU-funded projects already referred to. Respondents made written observations relating to ex-ternal pressure to change and the need for employee support for change. One respondent wrote that 'the issues facing our organisa-tion are flexibility, openness to change on all sides, and realising that the enemy is without and not within'. Another respondent stated that 'it was clear to management that the business was going to have lots of changes to make in order to keep on top of the com-petition ... so the 'working group' concept was introduced whereby a change required was determined by management ... and the group worked the change through to introduction'.

Another respondent commented that 'major resistance to change is not the shop floor but some senior managers who have risen in the ranks, know the system and have been rewarded by that system'. A number of respondents were cautious as to the likelihood of partnership delivering a new approach to organisa-tional change and this is taken up later in the section on outcomes.

Three-quarters of respondents from the eight public service bodies said that serious consumer/client pressures were either a very important or extremely important reason for adopting part-nership. Three quarters of respondents also said that anticipated significant future changes arising from governmental policies on organisation performance were either very important or ex-tremely important. Complying with a central agreement was said to be important by more than half (62.5 per cent) of respondents.

In summary, then, these findings appear to confirm the view that pressures relating to the competitive environment and/or to management-union-employee relationships play an important role in decisions to adopt partnership. At the same time, organisa-tions in Ireland appear to adopt partnership more as a planned approach to organisational change than as a response to an economic or relationships crisis.

Internal Influences on Adoption of Partnership

As seen already, although external pressures may generate the 'felt need' for partnership among employers and trade unions they do not in any sense 'determine' adoption. Internal factors such as employer and trade union values, trade union strength, the quality of relationships, the adequacy of the collective bargaining system, and the degree of support for partnership were also identified as factors likely to weigh heavily on decisions about partnership.

Presence and Role of Trade Unions

We saw in the international literature that adoption of partnership was associated with the presence of trade unions that had sufficient strength to ensure that they were not bypassed in the organisational change process (Cutcher-Gershenfeld and Verma, 1994). We also saw that strong trade unions might exert a degree of control over the development of partnership such as the membership of partnership bodies and the selection of agendas (Eaton, 1988; Roche and Turner, 1998; Marchington, 1992; Kelly, 2004).

In almost seven out of ten cases (69.4 per cent) all employees were included in the partnership arrangements but certain categories such as managerial, clerical, sales and marketing, professional or technical as well as non-union employees were excluded in 30.6 per cent of cases. Indeed, it is likely that many of these categories would not be unionised.

Almost nine out of ten respondents (88.1 per cent) put trade union density between 51 per cent and 100 per cent among those employees covered by the partnership arrangements (see Figure 4.4). In no case was trade union density less than 25 per cent.

Figure 4.4: Trade Union Density

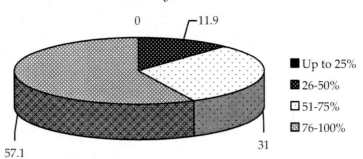

A little more than a tenth of those responding (11.9 per cent) said that trade union density was 26-50 per cent. Almost a third (31.0 per cent) said it was 51-75 per cent and more than half (57.1 per cent) said it was 76-100 per cent. Overall, then, the respondent organisations had a higher incidence of high trade union density than prevailed nationally. It might be expected, then, that these would be cases in which trade unions would have considerable influence.

About four out of ten organisations (43.9 per cent) had only one union in the partnership. A little less than a quarter (24.4 per cent) had two unions while less than one in ten (8.5 per cent) had three unions. A little less than a quarter (23.2 per cent) had four or more trade unions involved in partnership.

Having a number of unions might complicate the dynamics of partnership, for example by complicating agenda setting or by the effects of rivalry between unions. One respondent commented that 'we have four trade unions representing nearly 100 people and of these one union represents two people and another represents six people, these small groups tend to hold up progress'. Another commented that inter-union disagreement affected the establishment of a formal partnership forum.

While figures for union membership can indicate a certain degree of union strength at workplace level we considered it necessary to probe deeper in order to establish how active trade unions were. We asked respondents to describe the degree of trade union involvement in day-to-day plant operations such as staff deployment, redeployment and changes in job boundaries. The question assumes that where day-to-day involvement is high there will be a stronger likelihood that management would be motivated to secure trade union and employee co-operation with changes before these are implemented and vice versa. See Figure 4.5 below.

Figure 4.5: Degree of Trade Union Involvement

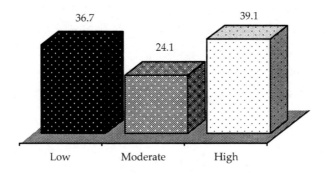

Almost four out of ten respondents (39.1 per cent) said that the degree of trade union involvement in day-to-day operations was high. Almost a quarter (24.1 per cent) said that it was moderate. More than a third (36.7 per cent) said that it was low.

We have no comparable findings from other surveys on levels of trade union involvement for comparison purposes. But it seems reasonable to conclude that the picture that emerges is one in which management might consider the unions concerned to have sufficient strength to warrant taking them seriously in the consideration of organisational changes. Given that almost six out of ten cases involved more than one trade union there is scope for different degrees of involvement by different trade unions but pursuing this was considered too complex for this investigation.

Taken together the findings relating to trade union density and trade union involvement in day to day operations appear to give broad support to the view that companies adopting partnership will have a high degree of trade union membership and involvement.

Quality of Management-Union-Employee Relationships

We have seen that organisations may develop partnership in order to improve poor current workplace relationships. We have also seen that having good current relationships can act as an encouragement to management and unions to seek to improve relationships further through partnership initiatives. We asked questions, therefore, about the quality of management-union relations, the level of trust between management and trade unions and the degree of employee support for change before the partnership initiatives had commenced. We set out the responses in Figure 4.6.

Figure 4.6: Management-Union-Employee Relations

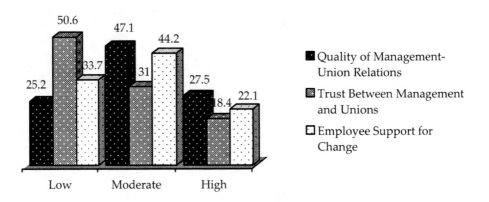

A quarter of respondents (25.2 per cent) said that the quality of management-union relations was low. About half (47.1 per cent) said it was moderate and a little more than a quarter (27.5 per cent) said it was high. Overall, almost three quarters of respondents (74.6 per cent) said that the quality of management-union relations was moderate or high.

The figures for the level of trust between management and trade unions before the establishment of partnership are less positive than for the quality of management-union relations. Slightly more than half of all respondents (50.6 per cent) said that trust was low. Slightly less than a third (31.0 per cent) said it was moderate and less than a fifth (18.4 per cent) said that the level of trust was high. Overall, eight out of ten respondents (81.6 per cent) said that the level of trust between management and unions was low to moderate. We have already seen that low trust is a defining feature of traditional, adversarial industrial relations. Distrust between management and unions tends to have deep roots and to act as a barrier to joint working (Cooke, 1990: 121-125).

A number of comments from respondents confirmed the importance of trust for the development of partnership. One respondent saw trust as a pre-condition of effective partnership in saying that 'our current situation is adversarial and trust needs to be rebuilt prior to effective partnership'. Another commented that 'our objective is to create a climate of trust where this partnership can develop to ensure the company remains competitive'. One very frank comment was that 'historically management determined behind closed doors the changes to be made in the business and presented a 'fait accompli' to the union reps – the result was inevitably confrontational resistance and a distrust of staff towards management'.

Slightly more than a third (33.7 per cent) said the degree of employee support for change was low. Close to a half (44.2 per cent) said it was moderate and less than a quarter (22.1 per cent) said the degree of employee support for change was high. Overall, almost eight out of ten respondents (77.9 per cent) said that the degree of employee support for change was low to moderate.

Taken together the figures for quality of management-union-employee relations, trust between management and trade unions and employee support for change, suggest that the overall quality of management-union-employee relationships might be described as low to moderate rather than moderate to high.

Adequacy of Collective Bargaining

We saw earlier that management and trade unions, in considering the adoption of partnership, appeared to take into account whether or not their current collective bargaining arrangements were adequate for handling industrial relations and organisational change issues (Rubin and Rubin, 2000). The line of thinking here was that if current collective bargaining arrangements were not adequate for handling mainstream industrial relations issues that the parties, and trade unions in particular, would not be disposed towards new forms of engagement but would concentrate on improving current bargaining arrangements. There was also an assumption here that one of the reasons for introducing a partnership approach to organisational change was that current collective bargaining arrangements were inadequate for handling such changes and that a more effective approach was needed. Figure 4.7 summarises the views of respondents on these issues.

There are striking differences in the perceptions of these managers as to the adequacy of their collective bargaining systems for the handling of industrial relations issues as opposed to organisational change issues. Almost three times as many respondents (34.2 per cent) rated collective bargaining as high in adequacy for handling industrial relations issues as rated it such for handling organisational change (12.8 per cent). Almost three times as many respondents (66.2 per cent) rated collective bargaining as low in adequacy for handling organisational change as rated it such for handling industrial relations issues (22.9 per cent).

Figure 4.7: Adequacy of Collective Bargaining Systems

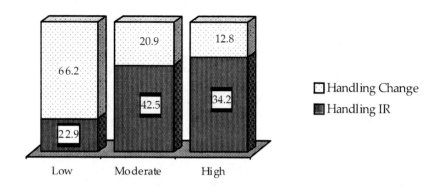

These findings appear to confirm strongly the proposition that where management and trade unions choose to adopt partnership there is likely to be a significant degree of satisfaction with the collective bargaining system as far as pay and conditions go but also a degree of dissatisfaction in regard to the handling of change through collective bargaining.

Management and Union Support for Partnership

We saw in the literature review that senior management and trade union support for partnership was important to success (Kochan and Dyer, 1976; Cohen-Rosenthal and Burton, 1987; Woodworth and Meek, 1994; HRDC, 1998). The argument was that senior and middle managers and trade union members would be motivated to support partnership to the extent that they saw visible commitment from the top. We also saw that senior managers and union officials could resolve difficulties arising at an operational level but needing decisions at a strategic level. We also saw that middle managers might be disposed against partnership because it might undermine their jobs and roles (Kochan et al., 1984; Fenton-O'Creevy, 1998; McKersie, 2002). We asked respondents, therefore, to describe the degree of support for partnership among top management, middle managers and full-time union officials. The responses for each category are set out in Figure 4.8.

The highest level of support for partnership appears among top managers. Almost seven out of ten of these (67.8 per cent) are reported as having high levels of support. Next are full-time union officials with more than half (55.2 per cent) being reported as having high levels of support. The lowest level of support appears to be among middle managers with less than four out of ten of these (38.2) having high levels of support. Full-time union officials appear to be more supportive of partnership than middle managers but not as supportive as senior managers.

Figure 4.8: Degree of Support for Partnership

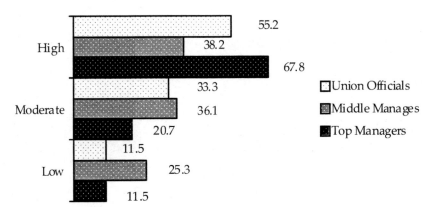

Some respondents were critical of the role of full-time officials. One respondent observed that certain union officials displayed a 'weakness in leadership and lack of common sense' and that in general 'grass-roots trade union members are not convinced that partnership is a good approach and as yet trade union officials have not succeeded in selling the concept to their members'. At the same time respondents acknowledged that effective partnership 'requires strong union/worker leadership'.

Employer Values and Human Resource Practices

The international literature suggested that employer espousal of 'employee oriented' values or policies could be an influence on the adoption of partnership (Kochan et al., 1984; Kochan and Osterman, 1994; Guest and Peccei, 2001). Such values might include a disposition towards consultation and information, a willingness to recognise and work with trade unions, guaranteeing employment security, direct involvement of employees, and commitment to training and development. All our respondents, by definition, recognised trade unions. In addition, the findings above show a significant degree of top management support for partnership

Less than a quarter of respondents (23.7 per cent) had single status for managers and other employees before partnership. A little more than a quarter (28.8 per cent) had guaranteed job security prior to partnership. Of the 23 cases that had guaranteed job security before partnership 15 were in the commercial state sector where such guarantees tend to apply anyway (Hastings, 1994) while only eight were in the private sector, five in mainly Irish-owned and three in foreign-owned companies. Of the 18 cases that had single status, eight were foreign-owned, six were state companies and four were mainly Irish-owned. These findings do not support the view that organisations that adopt partnership are likely to have 'employee oriented' policies like single status and guaranteed job security.

The incidence of different forms of employee communications prior to adoption of partnership is shown in Figure 4.9.

Almost seven out of ten respondents (69.0 per cent) said they had 'open door' policies. A majority also had team briefings (55.7 per cent) while almost half (46.6 per cent) said they used attitude surveys or suggestion schemes. A little more than half (53.6 per cent) had other, unspecified, employee communications schemes. Less than a quarter (24.7 per cent) had ways of empowering individual employees such as job enrichment. Communications practices such as these are categorised as 'direct involvement' (EFILWC, 1997; Frohlich and Pekruhl, 1996).

Figure 4.9: Communications Practices Prior to Partnership

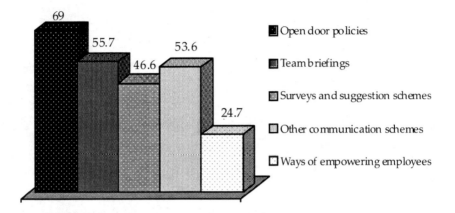

In Figure 4.10 we show the incidence of group involvement practices prior to adoption of partnership. Except for management-union working parties these practices would also be termed 'direct involvement' (EFILWC, 1997; Frohlich and Pekruhl, 1996). More than half of all respondents (56.5 per cent) had project groups or task forces.

Figure 4.10 Group Involvement Practices Prior to Partnership

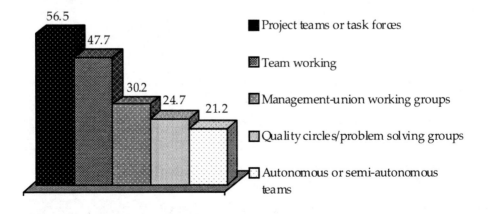

Slightly less than half of all respondents (47.7 per cent) had team working but that less than a quarter (21.2 per cent) had what might be termed 'strong' forms of teams such as autonomous or semi-autonomous teams. A little less than a third (30.2 per cent) had management-union working parties on specific issues while a little less than a quarter (24.7 per cent) had quality circles or problem solving groups.

While not directly comparable, it is worth noting that a 2003 survey found that less than four out of ten firms (39.3 per cent) with 50 or more employees had what were termed 'new work practices such as teamworking/multi-tasking/quality circles' (NCPP, 2004). The same survey found that almost three quarters of firms (74.1 per cent) with 50 or more employees had 'information to and consultation with staff on change in the company' and that about six out of ten (64.7 per cent) had 'arrangements for direct involvement of employees in decision making and problem solving (NCPP, 2004).

It would appear, then, that our respondent organisations did not have more advanced communications and involvement practices than the generality of companies and that they may, if anything, have been somewhat behind the generality of companies.

In Figure 4.11 we report the incidence of 'new rewards systems' that have been associated with partnership (Kochan and Osterman, 1994).

The incidence of new rewards systems appears quite low with less than a quarter of respondents indicating that they had any of the following in place before partnership: profit-related pay (23.5 per cent), employee share ownership schemes (23.5 per cent), individual (21.4 per cent) or group performance related pay (12.8 per cent), skills-based pay or 'save as you earn schemes' (16.9 per cent). The NCPP survey found that almost a third of firms with 50 or more employees (32.7 per cent) had 'profit sharing/share options/gain sharing for employees' (NCPP, 2004).

The evidence appears mixed but mainly negative on the assumption that human resource practices that reflect a management disposition towards employee and trade union involvement will be present beforehand in companies that adopt partnership. The incidence of guaranteed job security is certainly very low at 28.8 per cent, especially bearing in mind that the majority of cases with job security are from the commercial state sector. At the same time, such a low incidence may well reflect more the reality of private sector insecurity than any absence of employer values aimed at improving the security of employees.

Figure 4.11: Pay-related HR Practices Prior to Partnership

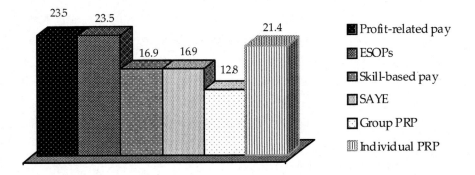

The incidence of new reward systems such as profit-related pay and ESOPs that might be regarded as supportive of partnership is also certainly low. On the other hand, there is a reasonably high incidence of certain HR practices, notably project groups, formal training for employees and open door policies. As already seen, the literature also suggests that these HR practices might be introduced after partnership is adopted. The findings on agendas that are discussed in the next chapter will facilitate further exploration of this issue.

Summary and Conclusions

Most of the organisations that took part in the survey were in the manufacturing sector, were mature in age terms and had large numbers of employees. Most were foreign-owned. The vast majority of cases were established between 1997 and 2000. It is clear that a number of these arose in the context of local pay and change agreements or from company involvement in the EU-funded partnership projects being sponsored by IBEC, ICTU, IPC and SIPTU. The number of respondents from the public services was small because of a research decision to exclude cases that were not 'voluntary' in our sense of the term. Most partnership arrangements were grounded in industrial relations in that they were jointly initiated, were subject to a formal agreement and were highly inclusive of different categories of employees.

The findings appear to confirm the view that pressures relating to the competitive environment and/or to management-union-employee relationships played an important role in decisions to adopt partnership. The most important reason for adopting partnership was, however, the anticipation of significant future changes in respondents' commercial situation for which they wanted to prepare the organisation. The extent to which organisations in Ireland appeared to adopt partnership as a response to an economic or relationships crisis seems lower than might be suggested by the international literature.

Taken together the findings relating to trade union density and trade union involvement in day to day operations confirm the view that companies adopting partnership were likely to have a high degree of trade union membership and involvement. In addition, the findings also show that the overall quality of management-union-employee relationships could be described as low to moderate rather than moderate to high.

The findings appear to confirm that before management and trade unions adopt partnership they need to be satisfied that the collective bargaining system is adequate for handling pay and conditions but not as adequate for handling organisational change. In organisations adopting partnership there is likely to be a moderate to high degree of support for partnership among managers and full-time union officials.

Finally, the evidence appears mixed but mainly negative with respect to the view that certain 'employee-oriented' human resource practices will be found beforehand in companies that adopt partnership. In the next chapter we describe in detail how these partnership arrangements operated. We pay particular attention to how they were structured and to the agendas that the parties addressed through them.

5

Partnership in Practice

This chapter provides a detailed account of the structures and agendas that organisations developed in order to put partnership into practice. In the survey we gathered data on strategic partnership bodies, operational partnership bodies and bodies such as working groups, project teams etc. We also gathered data on the strategic and operational agendas that had been addressed through these bodies and we asked respondents to rank agenda items in order of priority. We begin the account with an outline of what structures were in place and how they operated. Then we outline the agendas that were worked on through these structures.

Partnership Structures

Numbers of Strategic and Operational Partnership Bodies

We defined strategic partnership bodies as management-union groups that were mainly focused on corporate issues such as new products or services, business plans, major changes relating to changes in pay, working conditions and working practices, changes in ownership etc. We defined operational partnership bodies as management-union groups that were mainly focused on day-to-day issues such as work practices, work organisation, rosters, product quality, day-to-day problems etc. Because we expected that responding organisations would have a number of strategic and operational partnership bodies we did not consider it feasible to gather detailed information on all such bodies. Instead, we asked respondents to give information in respect to the strategic and/or operational partnership body that they considered had made the most important contribution to the organisation so far. We discuss the operational aspects of the strategic and operational partnership bodies together as it will be seen that there are more similarities than differences in terms of their basic operations. More than half of all respondents (59.8 per cent) said they had strategic partnership bodies and more than eight out of ten (83.7 per cent) said they had operational partnership bodies.

Figure 5.1: Numbers of Partnership Bodies

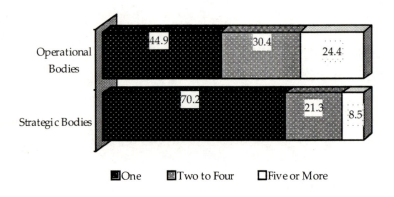

There were 86 strategic partnership bodies in total. As might be expected, in the majority of cases (70.2 per cent) respondents had a single strategic partnership body (see Figure 5.1). Less than one in four (21.3 per cent) had two to four strategic bodies and 8.5 per cent had five or more strategic bodies. In total there were 213 operational partnership bodies. As might be expected, the incidence of multiple operational bodies was greater than the incidence of multiple strategic bodies. Less than half the respondents (44.9 per cent) had a single operational body while 30.4 per cent had two to four and 24.4 per cent had five or more operational bodies.

We had thought that the incidence of strategic partnership bodies would be influenced by the degree of trade union strength in the organisation, the assumption being that the stronger the trade union the greater the likelihood of it succeeding in having influence at this level. This did not turn out to be the case.

Levels at Which Partnership Bodies Operated

In Figure 5.2 we show the distribution of strategic and operational partnership bodies at different levels of organisation. As might be expected, the incidence of strategic bodies is higher at corporate level than at workplace level whereas the incidence of operational bodies is higher at workplace level than at corporate level.

Almost half the respondents (47.1 per cent) said the strategic bodies were operating at corporate level, 31.4 per cent at business unit level and 25.5 per cent at workplace level. Only a handful of respondents (5.6 per cent) said that the operational bodies were operating at corporate level, 31.9 per cent said at business unit level and almost seven out of ten (69.4 per cent) said the operational partnership bodies were operating at workplace level.

Figure 5.2: Levels at Which Partnership Bodies Operated

	Corporate	Business Unit	Workplace
Operational Bodies	5.6	31.9	69.4
Strategic Bodies	47.1	31.4	25.5

Titles of Partnership Bodies

The most common titles for strategic and operational bodies lend insights into the agendas or purposes of these bodies. Common titles for strategic bodies were 'business process improvement', 'continuous improvement', 'communications', 'WCM task force', 'new work organisation steering group' etc. In other cases more generic titles were used such as 'consultative group', 'corporate partnership forum', 'national employee participation forum', 'partnership committee', 'steering committee' etc.

Operational partnership bodies had titles such as 'annual hours team', 'change to compete team', 'continuous improvement steering team', 'delivery channel review group', 'process improvement team' etc. In other cases more generic titles were used such as 'works committee', 'company-union council', 'joint working party', 'partnership forum', 'steering committee' etc.

Chairing and Membership

Given that management and trade unions jointly initiated many of these partnership arrangements it might be expected that they would share the chairing role. Managers chaired slightly less than half (47.0 per cent) of all operational and strategic partnership bodies. Slightly more than half (51.0 per cent) were jointly chaired or chaired in rotation. Almost half of the strategic bodies (46.2 per cent) and slightly less of the operational bodies (37.7 per cent) had equal numbers of management and union members. As might be expected, there were many cases where there were more union than management members.

Management Members

There were significant differences between the management memberships of strategic and operational partnership bodies, as seen in Figure 5.3. As might be expected, chief executive officers were twice as likely to be on strategic bodies (40.4 per cent) as on operational ones (18.3 per cent). Top IR/HR managers were also more likely to be on strategic bodies (80.8 per cent) than on operational ones (46.5 per cent). On the other hand, the membership of other senior executives was very high on both strategic bodies (88.5 per cent) and on operational ones (70.4 per cent). Again, as might be expected, the incidence of line managers was higher on operational bodies (69.0 per cent) than on strategic ones (42.3 per cent) as was the incidence of supervisors (35.2 and 28.8 respectively).

Figure 5.3: Management Participation on Partnership Bodies

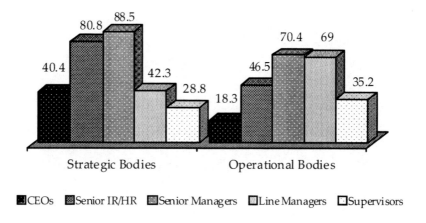

Line managers and supervisors are the least well represented on both strategic and operational partnership bodies. Given that parties who take part in partnership tend to have more positive attitudes to it than those who don't, this may partly explain the lower levels of support for partnership among middle as opposed to top management, as seen in the last chapter. We had thought that the incidence of chief executive or other top manager membership of partnership bodies would be influenced by the degree of trade union strength in the organisations concerned. This did not turn out to be the case.

Trade Union and Employee Members

There is less variation in the trade union and employee membership of strategic and operational partnership bodies, as seen in Figure 5.4. As might be expected, the incidence of involvement by full-time officials is higher on strategic bodies (61.5 per cent) than

on operational ones (42.3). On the other hand, there is no significant difference between the shop steward presence on strategic
partnership bodies (84.6 per cent) and operational ones (81.7).

Figure 5.4: Trade Union Participation on Partnership Bodies

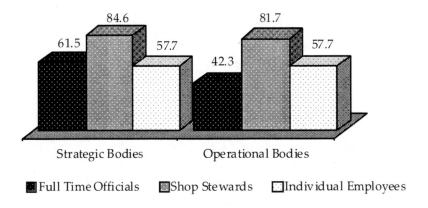

Perhaps surprisingly, given the highly unionised character of
these organisations, individual employees were present on more
than half of both strategic and operational partnership bodies
(57.7 per cent in both cases). These findings do not confirm that
involvement of full-time officials happens at the expense of shop
stewards as might be suggested by some of the critics of partnership (Marks et al., 1998; Kelly, 2004).

Frequency and Duration of Meetings

The majority of strategic and operational partnership bodies met
monthly or every two to three months, as seen in Figure 5.5.

About four out of ten strategic (43.2 per cent) and operational
(42.1 per cent) bodies met every three to four weeks. About three
out of ten strategic (33.3 per cent) and operational (31.9 per cent)
bodies met every two to three months. As might be expected
given the types of issues they would be dealing with, more operational bodies (23.1 per cent) than strategic bodies (7.9 per cent)
met every one to two weeks.

Figure 5.5: Frequency of Meetings

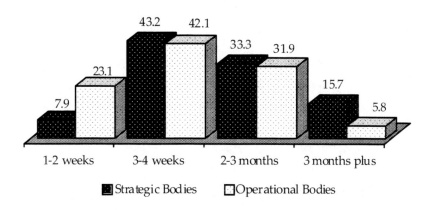

About a third (35.3 per cent) of operational partnership bodies met for an hour at a time compared to 13.7 per cent of strategic bodies. On the other hand, more than half (51.0 per cent) of the strategic bodies met for between one and two hours compared to less than a third (32.4 per cent) of operational bodies. Almost a third (29.4 per cent) of strategic bodies and 27.9 per cent of operational bodies met for between two and three hours. The incidence of meetings that lasted longer than three hours was quite low, 5.9 per cent for strategic bodies and 4.4 per cent for operational bodies.

Facilitation and Training Arrangements

The 'how to' literature on partnership assigned importance to the training of partnership committee members, to the role that facilitators could play in helping groups to develop and to the importance of keeping the wider workforce informed of developments through separate and joint communications. A majority of participants in both strategic and operational partnership bodies received training. Joint training was provided for about half of all operational bodies (47.1 per cent) and for slightly fewer strategic bodies (41.2 per cent). Separate training was provided in the case of 10.3 per cent of operational bodies and 13.7 per cent of strategic bodies. Significant minorities of both operational (42.6 per cent) and strategic bodies (45.1 per cent) received no training at all.

Most partnership bodies did not have facilitators at their meetings: 72.1 per cent of operational bodies and 55.8 per cent of strategic bodies. The attendance by facilitators at all meetings was higher for strategic bodies (21.2 per cent) than for operational bodies (8.8 per cent) as was the incidence of attendance at some meetings, 23.1 per cent of strategic body meetings and 19.1 per cent for operational body meetings.

In Exhibit 5.1 we give a brief description of the roles of training, relationships building and communications in the development of partnership at ANORD Control Systems Ltd, a manufacturer of electrical control switchboards and process control equipment based in Dundalk since 1969 (IPC, 1999). This was one of ten companies in the EU-funded IPC-IBEC-ICTU programme titled *New Work Organisation in Ireland* (NWO). Other companies were: Kingspan, Atlas Aluminium, Tara Mines, SIFA, SIGMA, Tegral Metal Forming, Musgrave Supervalu–Centra, Henkel, and Honeywell-Measurex (Totterdill and Sharpe, 1999). The objective of the programme was to help companies introduce 'good/best practices' in work organisation through joint management-union structures and activities in keeping with *Partnership 2000*. The types of changes concerned in this case would traditionally have to be agreed through collective bargaining.

Exhibit 5.1: ANORD Control Systems Ltd.

In the mid-1990s, ANORD's competitive position was weakened by confrontational industrial relations arising from pay demands that the company could not satisfy without radical restructuring. Following a Labour Court intervention, the company, its unions – SIPTU and TEEU - and ICTU negotiated a partnership agreement that provided for a joint committee on 'world class manufacturing' (WCM). Partnership was intended to improve security of employment, facilitate manufacturing teamwork, and deliver harmonious industrial relations. When the company and unions joined the NWO Programme they established a joint 'steering group' that was representative of a 'diagonal slice' of the organisation. The role of this group was to identify projects, establish 'task teams' to implement projects, support the work of the task teams, and communicate developments to the wider organisation. Projects were designed to last 12-16 weeks to be most effective. Two external facilitators from IPC worked with the group. Training in problem solving, meetings, teamwork and communications was provided to the 'steering group' and teamwork training, training in WCM, and team leadership was provided to the 'task teams'. Training programmes offered opportunities for relationships building as did internal and external 'learning networks'. The IPC carried out an organisational diagnostic review the findings of which formed the initial agenda for the 'steering group'. Communications had traditionally been poor and initiatives to address this included the 'steering group' and 'task teams' themselves, a staff survey, noticeboards, bulletins from the 'steering group' and presentations to all staff. Manufacturing teams were established that allowed for some devolution of decision-making and for more employee responsibility. In-company facilitators were trained to sustain the momentum for change after the NWO programme had ended.

The ANORD case appears to illustrate a number of important points about organisational change in unionised settings, particularly changes in work organisation in the manufacturing sector (Dawson, 1994; Neumann et al., 1995). To state the obvious, unions are not necessarily opposed to change and can be effective allies of management in bringing about changes. But they are unlikely to do this solely on terms that management set. We saw earlier that partnership as an approach to organisational change provides a structured mechanism through which union representatives can table the interests or goals of employees alongside management interests and goals.

The ANORD collective agreements on WCM and on joining the NWO programme can be seen as the type of 'enabling agreements' that can facilitate organisational change by assuring employees that they are not being disadvantaged and by helping them to be open and confident about change. The partnership arrangements themselves, the 'steering group' and 'task teams', also provided an important context within which changes could be introduced with high levels of employee and trade union involvement. The structures provided for involvement at both operational or 'task' levels and at a higher 'steering group' level where difficulties could be discussed and resolved with the involvement of senior union representatives. The initial IPC diagnostic provided the 'steering group' – the 'champions' of the change process – with information on factors likely to hinder and help the change process and on issues that needed to be addressed to satisfy management and employee interests or goals.

The case also illustrates the importance of addressing industrial relations issues as part of the change process and of continuously improving employee relations and trust levels. We saw earlier that adversarial relationships were antipathetic to the effective introduction of new work systems (ICTU, 1993: 16). We also saw that employee involvement in problem-solving groups and teams cannot be taken for granted where there has been low involvement and low trust (Kochan and Osterman, 1994; Regini, 1995).

Communications from Partnership Bodies

We also saw in the literature review that partnership provided opportunities for management and trade unions to improve communications. Joint communications represent a departure for both management and trade unions from the communications patterns within 'arms length' industrial relations. Traditionally management would either communicate directly with the workforce or would do so through the trade unions while trade unions would communicate directly with their own members.

The majority of partnership bodies, however, issued either occasional or frequent joint communications to the workforce. Almost half (48.0 per cent) of the strategic bodies and slightly less of the operational bodies (42.6 per cent) issued occasional joint communications. On the other hand, 30.9 per cent of operational bodies issued regular joint communications as opposed to 24.0 per cent of strategic bodies. In a minority of cases (28.0 per cent of strategic bodies and 26.5 per cent of operational bodies) there were no joint communications and management and trade unions made all communications separately. These findings suggest a high degree of openness on the part of management and trade unions to experiment with new forms of communication that might be seen as 'risky' given their traditional patterns of separate communication with the workforce and trade union members.

Other Forms of Employee Involvement

In the previous chapter we noted that respondent organisations did not have a high incidence of employee involvement practices prior to adoption of partnership. We saw in the literature review that such practices might be present before partnership was adopted or they might be developed as a consequence of partnership. We asked, therefore, about other forms of employee and trade union involvement that had been introduced under the aegis of partnership. Figure 5.6 shows the extent to which such practices were introduced under the aegis of partnership alongside the incidence of these practices prior to the establishment of partnership.

The incidence of project groups prior to partnership (56.5 per cent) was significantly higher than the introduction of such groups under the aegis of partnership (27.7 per cent). The incidence of team working prior to partnership (47.7 per cent) was also significantly higher than the introduction of team working under the aegis of partnership (24.4 per cent). On the other hand, the figures for the introduction of management-union working parties under the aegis of partnership were greater (44.2 per cent) than for before partnership (30.2 per cent). The findings relating to autonomous teams and quality circles are not that different.

Figure 5.6: Employee Involvement Practices Under Partnership

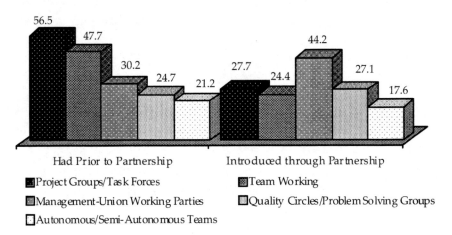

Only in the case of management-union working parties do the findings show a higher incidence after than prior to partnership. This may reflect a cautious approach on the part of management and unions towards the expansion of direct involvement in circumstances where the parties have only recently begun implementing new forms of representative involvement (Cutcher-Gershenfeld and Verma, 1994).

Overall Forms of Partnership

In the literature review we saw that there was imprecision as to what exactly 'partnership' meant in the management-union context. We included in the survey four statements as to how partnership mainly worked in terms of decision-making. We asked respondents to indicate which of the statements described most closely how partnership mainly worked in their organisations. Table 5.1 sets out the statements and the responses.

Table 5.1: Overall Forms of Partnership

Overall Form that Partnership Takes	% Responses
1. Partnership in our organisation is mostly about management and unions tentatively exploring new ways of working together without yet having agreed definitions as to what issues might be addressed, what the new roles of managers and representatives might be or what structures might be developed to give effect to these new roles	30.4
2. Partnership in our organisation is mostly a means through which the management and unions can formulate recommendations that then go to management and the unions for decision or negotiation through the established management and union decision making processes	30.4
3. Partnership in our organisation is mostly about management keeping the unions up to date with management's plans through structures that facilitate information and consultation and which otherwise leave decision making to management	26.6
4. Partnership in our organisation involves managers and union representatives making joint decisions that are then implemented by both parties	12.7

A little less than a third of respondents (30.4 per cent) selected the first statement, which described a form of partnership in which the parties have yet to make significant boundary changes relating to management and trade union decision-making (Roche and Turner, 1998). A little less than a third of respondents (30.4 per cent) selected the second statement, which described a form of partnership in which the parties have decided to work together on certain issues through partnership but with final decisions having to be made through managerial decision-making and collective bargaining, as appropriate.

Slightly more than a quarter (26.6 per cent) selected the third statement, which described a form of partnership which is based around information and consultation and without interference with existing decision-making systems. The least frequently selected statement at 12.7 per cent was the fourth which described 'joint decision-making' in which final decisions are made within the partnership process without the parties having to ratify them through managerial decision-making or collective bargaining or union voting (Cutcher-Gershenfeld and Verma, 1994; Roche and Turner, 1998). This form of partnership would be considered as one of the 'strongest' within the literature (Roche and Turner, 1998).

It is not surprising that only a small minority designated their partnerships as 'joint decision-making' given the recent provenance of the cases. We saw in Chapter 3 that adopting partnership involves considerable risks for both employers and trade unions. It might be expected, then, that 'strong' forms of partnership would only arise in a limited number of instances. It is also to be expected that given the adversarial backgrounds to many of the cases that employers and trade unions would continue to rely to a high degree on managerial decision-making and collective bargaining for bringing issues to finality. It is also worth noting that many multinational subsidiaries in Ireland have only a limited degree of decision-making autonomy anyway (IRN, 7 July 2005).

Finally, we had thought that that the incidence of the different forms of partnership would be influenced by trade union strength, i.e. that 'strong' forms such as joint decision-making would be more common in companies with high levels of trade union membership. The findings did not bear this out.

Partnership Agendas

Deciding on Agendas

Almost eight out of ten respondents (79.0 per cent) said the partnership agenda reflected the concerns of each side equally. Only
14.0 per cent said agendas reflected more the concerns of management and only 8.0 per cent said agendas reflected more the
concerns of trade unions. See Figure 5.7. These findings suggest a
strong 'mutual gains' dimension to partnership agendas. This,
however, is a management response and it needs to be considered
in the context of the more detailed responses about agendas,
which we discuss below.

Figure 5.7: Mutual Gains Agenda

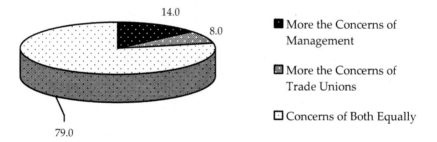

In about nine out of ten cases (96.2 per cent for strategic and
89.9 per cent for operational bodies) management and unions both
decided what went on the agenda. In about nine out of ten cases
(90.4 per cent for both strategic and operational bodies) there was
usually a formal agenda for each meeting.

Strategic Partnership Agendas

We asked respondents to provide agenda information in respect
to the strategic partnership body that they considered had made
the most important contribution to the organisation so far. We
present the responses in Table 5.2.

Table 5.2: Agendas: Strategic Partnership Bodies

	Discussed in Past Six Months %	Ranked in Order of Importance
The financial performance of the organisation	69.2	1
The competitive position of the organisation	69.2	2
Business plans	65.4	3
Cost savings	51.9	4
Plans regarding major changes in work practices	55.8	5
Plans relating to the redesign of pay systems	32.7	6
The level of service to customers/clients	51.9	7
Relations between managers/supervisors and employee/representatives	42.3	8
Health and safety systems	46.2	9
Introduction of new products or services	57.7	10
Introduction of new organisation structures	44.2	11
Discussion of company plans to develop gain sharing	36.5	12
Personnel and industrial relations procedures and practices	34.6	13
Strategic training plans	30.8	14
Introduction of new technology/machinery	46.2	15
Plans to introduce new forms of work organisation	38.5	16
Plans relating to significant adjustments to grading systems	25.0	17
Changes in ownership of the organisation	26.9	18
Reviewing staffing levels	25.0	19
Job security	23.1	20

The three items listed most frequently as having been discussed within the past six months were the financial performance of the organisation (69.2 per cent), the competitive position of the organisation (69.2 per cent), and business plans (65.4 per cent).

These three items were also ranked highest in importance, using a system of weighted voting (i.e. giving five points to items ranked first in order of importance down to one point for items ranked fifth in order of importance).

The next most commonly discussed items were the introduction of new products or services (57.7 per cent), ranked tenth in importance; plans regarding major changes in work practice (55.8 per cent), ranked fifth in importance; cost savings (51.9 per cent), ranked fourth in importance; and the level of service provided to customers/clients (51.9 per cent), ranked seventh in importance.

More than four out of ten respondents had discussed health and safety systems (46.2 per cent), introduction of new technology/machinery (46.2 per cent), introduction of new organisation structures (44.2 per cent) and relations between managers and supervisors and employees and representatives (42.3 per cent). About a third of all those responding had discussed plans to introduce new forms of work organisation (38.5 per cent), company plans to develop gain sharing (36.5 per cent), industrial relations procedures and practices (34.6 per cent), plans relating to the redesign of pay systems (32.7 per cent) and strategic training plans (30.8 per cent). About a quarter of those responding had discussed changes in ownership of the organisation (26.9 per cent), plans relating to significant adjustments to grading systems (25.0 per cent), reviewing staffing levels (25.0 per cent) and job security (23.1 per cent).

Taken together the top half of Table 5.2 constitutes a strategic partnership agenda that has a strong focus on what might be termed the traditional business concerns of top management. What, however, do these findings reveal about the degree to which the strategic partnership agenda reflects employee and trade union interests, the 'mutual gains' dimension?

Two traditional employee concerns featured in the top ten in order of importance. Relations between managers and supervisors and employees and representatives were discussed in 42.3 per cent of cases and were ranked eighth in order of importance.

Health and safety was discussed in 46.2 per cent of cases and was ranked ninth in order of importance. Discussion of company plans to develop gain sharing was discussed in more than a third (36.5 per cent) of all cases but was ranked at twelfth position in order of importance. Another traditional employee concern, training, was discussed in 30.8 per cent of cases and was ranked fourteenth in order of importance.

Perhaps the issue of most concern to employees and trade unions is job security. This was the least frequently discussed agenda item at 23.1 per cent. It was also ranked as the least important.

Taken together, the findings suggest that the strategic partnership agenda is weighted towards employer concerns and that there is a 'mutual gains' deficit. On the other hand, it might be argued that because the agenda is strongly focused on business concerns that it provides opportunities to trade unions and employees to influence this agenda in ways that would not be available were the agenda to focus more on employee concerns. It may be the case that trade union and employee concerns are more likely to feature on operational partnership agendas than on strategic ones and it is to this issue that the discussion will now turn.

Operational Partnership Agendas

We present the responses relating to operational partnership agendas in Table 5.3. The three items listed most frequently as having been discussed within the past six months on the operational partnership agenda were implementation of changes in work practices (72.2 per cent), industrial relations grievances raised by employees/representatives (55.6 per cent), and the financial performance of the organisation (52.8 per cent). These also feature in the top three as ranked in order of importance.

Table 5.3: Agendas: Operational Partnership Bodies

	Discussed in Past Six Months %	Ranked in Order of Importance
Implementation of changes in work practices	72.2	1
The financial performance of the organisation	52.8	2
IR grievances raised by employees/representatives	55.6	3
Introduction of new technology/machinery	50.0	4
Introduction of new organisation structures	51.4	5
Proposals relating to pay systems	41.7	6
Gain sharing	38.9	7
Relations between managers/supervisors and employees/representatives	47.2	8
Management-union-employee communications	51.4	9
Cost savings	50.0	10
Health and safety issues	50.0	11
Job security	33.3	12
The level of service to customers/clients	38.9	13
New forms of work organisation	47.2	14
The implementation of business plans	33.3	15
Personnel and industrial relations procedures and practices	48.6	16
Training	52.8	17
Introduction of new products or services	37.5	18
Changes in ownership of the organisation	20.8	19
Canteen facilities and services	45.8	20
Rosters and leave	37.5	21
Staffing levels	34.7	22
Proposals relating to grading systems	16.7	23
Fringe benefits such as holiday concessions, medical services	52.8	24
Social and recreational activities and facilities	27.8	25
Equality issues	15.3	26

The next most frequently discussed were training and fringe benefits such as holiday concessions and medical services (both 52.8 per cent) with the former being ranked seventeenth and the latter twenty-fourth. Next in order of frequency of discussion were the introduction of new organisation structures and man-agement-union-employee communications (both 51.4 per cent) with the former being ranked fourth and the latter ninth. Half of all respondents (50.0 per cent) said they had discussed the intro-duction of new technology/machinery in the past six months, ranked fourth in order of importance; cost savings, ranked tenth; and health and safety issues, ranked eleventh.

Issues discussed in more than four out of ten cases were per-sonnel and industrial relations procedures and practices (48.6 per cent), ranked sixteenth in order of importance; relations between managers/supervisors and employees/representatives (47.2 per cent), ranked eighth; new forms of work organisation (47.2 per cent), ranked fourteenth; canteen facilities and services (45.8 per cent), ranked twentieth; and proposals relating to pay systems (41.7 per cent), ranked sixth.

A third or more of respondents said they had discussed the level of service to customers/clients (38.9 per cent), ranked thir-teenth in order of importance; introduction of new products or services (37.5 per cent), ranked eighteenth; rosters and leave (37.5 per cent), ranked twenty-first; staffing levels (34.7 per cent), ranked twenty-second; job security (33.3 per cent), ranked twelfth; and the implementation of business plans (33.3 per cent), ranked fifteenth.

The least frequently discussed operational partnership agenda items were social and recreational activities and facilities (27.8 per cent), ranked second last in order of importance; changes in own-ership of the organisation (20.8 per cent), ranked nineteenth; pro-posals relating to grading systems (16.7 per cent), ranked twenty-third; and equality issues (15.3 per cent), ranked last.

Taken together, the top half of Table 5.3 constitutes an operational partnership agenda that is focused strongly on the traditional business concerns of operational management. What, however, does the table indicate regarding the concerns of employees and trade unions?

Job security features higher in importance than on the strategic partnership agenda, albeit towards the end of the upper half. Gain sharing was ranked seventh in order of importance and relations between managers and supervisors and employees and representatives was ranked eighth. Management-union-employee communications ranked ninth in order of importance and health and safety systems ranked twelfth. Overall, then, it appears reasonable to conclude that the operational partnership agenda reflects traditional employee and trade union concerns more strongly than the strategic partnership agenda. At the same time it also appears reasonable to conclude that there is also a significant 'mutual gains' deficit at operational partnership agenda level.

It is worth noting the extent to which there is an overlap between the ten items most frequently discussed on both the strategic and operational partnership agendas. Five headings are common to the two lists: the financial performance of the organisation, cost savings, changes in work practices, pay systems, and relations between managers and supervisors and employees and representatives. This is not surprising given that it might be expected that issues that were decided at the level of strategic partnership bodies would then move down to operational partnership levels for further discussion and/or for implementation.

Exclusion of Industrial Relations Issues

We saw from the literature review that many commentators argued that partnership and industrial relations agendas should be kept separate, at least initially (Kochan et al., 1984). On the other hand, there were commentators who argued that such a separation was a convenient fiction and that the overlap between partnership and collective bargaining was inevitable (Rankin and Mansell, 1986). There are certain issues that may be considered to be 'generic' industrial relations issues in unionised companies such as pay and grading systems, changes in work practices and new forms of work organisation, introduction of new technology and machinery, personnel and industrial relations procedures and practices, and staffing levels and cost savings. It seems reasonable to expect that significant developments under these headings would be handled through negotiation with trade unions.

In Table 5.4 we show the extent to which a range of such issues had been discussed at corporate and operational partnership bodies in the six months prior to completion of the questionnaire.

Table 5.4: IR Issues on Partnership Agendas

	Strategic Partnership Bodies %	Operational Partnership Bodies %
Changes in work practices	55.8	72.2
Cost savings	51.9	50.0
New technology/machinery	46.2	50.0
New forms of work organisation	38.5	47.2
Gain sharing	36.5	38.9
IR procedures and practices	34.6	48.6
Pay systems	32.7	41.7
Grading systems	25.0	16.7
Staffing levels	25.0	34.7

More than half of those responding said they had discussed changes in work practices at strategic bodies (55.8 per cent) and almost three quarters at operational bodies (72.2 per cent). More than half also said they had discussed cost savings at strategic bodies (51.9 per cent) and exactly half at operational bodies (50.0 per cent). More than four out of ten (46.2) had discussed new technology/machinery at strategic bodies and 50.0 per cent at operational bodies. More than a third had discussed new forms of work organisation at strategic bodies (38.5 per cent) and 47.2 per cent at operational bodies.

Gain sharing had been on the agendas of more than a third of all strategic (36.5 per cent) and operational (38.9 per cent) partnership agendas. Industrial relations procedures and practices featured on more than a third (34.6 per cent) of strategic partnership bodies and on almost half (48.6 per cent) of all operational bodies. Pay systems were discussed on almost a third of all strategic bodies (32.7 per cent) and on four out of ten operational bodies (41.7 per cent). Only a quarter of respondents (25.0 per cent) said that grading systems had been on the strategic agenda and only 16.7 per cent said it had been on the operational agenda. Finally, staffing levels featured on a quarter of strategic bodies (25.0 per cent) and on a third (34.7 per cent) of operational bodies.

What conclusions might reasonably be drawn from these findings? It seems reasonable to conclude that not alone are industrial relations issues not precluded from strategic and operational partnership agendas but that they feature to a reasonable degree, perhaps to a greater extent on operational than on strategic agendas. What the data do not tell us, however, is what happened to these agenda items at these partnership bodies. For example, the parties may have agreed to their inclusion on partnership agendas on the basis that they will be discussed there in an initial fashion and then transferred to the collective bargaining agenda for negotiation. However, it would seem unreasonable to assume that this would happen in all cases.

While the effects of partnership on collective bargaining will be discussed in greater detail in the next chapter it is worth citing one particular finding here. When asked had issues that were previously handled through collective bargaining been passed into the partnership system more than a quarter of those respond-ing (28.4 per cent) said that they had not. More than a third (40.7 per cent), however, said that minor issues had been transferred and almost another third (30.7 per cent) said that major issues had been transferred from collective bargaining to partnership. This suggests that at least in a significant minority of cases the parties agreed to handle major industrial relations issues in a non-adversarial manner through partnership. This appears to repre-sent a significant attempt to overcome the limitations of tradi-tional, adversarial collective bargaining.

Influence of Main Driving Forces on Agendas

We had thought that the main driving forces for the adoption of partnership would influence partnership agendas. For example, we thought that the more serious the commercial pressures on an organisation were, the more the partnership agenda might ad-dress issues that, handled successfully, might help to reduce that degree of commercial pressure. We were thinking of agendas such as cost savings, new forms of work organisations, changes in work practices and in pay systems etc. However, when we tested for this there was no strong association between the reasons given for adopting partnership and the types of agendas listed.

Influence of Trade Union Strength on Agendas

We had also thought that the degree of trade union strength as indicated by membership levels would influence the partnership agenda. For example, we expected that in cases where there was a very high degree of trade union membership there would be a strong focus on issues of concern to employees and trade unions. The assumption here was that employers would be more likely to accommodate the interests of strong as opposed to weak trade unions. However, when we tested for this there was no strong as-sociation between trade union strength and agendas.

Summary and Conclusions

In this chapter we saw that there was a high incidence of strategic partnership bodies – about six out of ten cases had these. Not surprisingly, there was a higher incidence of operational bodies. In most cases there was joint agenda setting and joint chairing.

Only a small minority of cases reported that they had joint decision-making. There were high incidences of partnerships that relied on final decisions being made separately by management and trade unions and that mainly took the form of information and consultation. It seems that in most cases management and trade unions wanted to retain pre-established ways of making decisions affecting them both. There was no evidence that trade union strength influenced the form of partnership developed.

Both strategic and operational agendas included issues of substance for the most part. There was also a high degree of commonality between the strategic and operational partnership agendas, for example around issues such as financial performance, changes in work practices etc. Partnership agendas were focused to a greater degree on issues of concern to management than to trade unions and employees. There was no evidence that trade union strength influenced the content of either strategic or operational partnership agendas.

Industrial relations issues were present to a significant degree on partnership agendas. For example, industrial relations grievances appeared third in frequency and importance on operational agendas. It seems that partnership agendas were skewed somewhat towards a management rather than an employee or trade union agenda. Whether more benefits accrued to management than to employees or trade unions is an issue that will be discussed in the next chapter.

6

OUTCOMES FOR EMPLOYERS, EMPLOYEES AND TRADE UNIONS

In this chapter we provide the most detailed account to date of conclusions that senior managers in Ireland have come to on the outcomes of partnership initiatives in their organisations. As already seen, in most cases these were senior human resource executives and in some cases they were general or production managers. Because so many of these initiatives were still in their early stages we did not consider it reasonable to expect managers to provide definitive judgments on the outcomes of partnership. For that reason we asked about outcomes currently achieved due to the influence of partnership as well as outcomes expected over the coming five years. We begin the chapter with a discussion of outcomes of particular importance to employers. Then we discuss outcomes of particular importance to employees. Next we discuss the findings relating directly to trade unions. We then discuss outcomes affecting all parties. Finally, we consider how partnership has affected industrial relations and the levels of support for partnership among managers and shop stewards.

Outcomes for Employers

The outcomes of particular interest to employers that we sought to measure were business performance, union members' attitudes, and how partnership affects decision-making.

Business Performance and Workforce Productivity

Employers are likely to have the greatest interest in economic or 'bottom line' outcomes (Cooke, 1990). Specific economic outcomes such as changes in labour costs per unit of output or profits per unit of sales require access to organisation records over a period of time. We did not consider it feasible to expect managers to take such detailed information into account let alone make it available in a postal survey. For that reason we included two broad questions on current and expected future changes in organisational performance in those parts of the organisation covered by partnership, one on business performance and one on workforce productivity. We summarise the findings in Figure 6.1.

Figure 6.1: Effects on Business and Productivity

Almost two-thirds (64.4 per cent) of the managers said that current business performance was higher in those parts of the organisation covered by partnership due to the influence of partnership. Slightly more than a third (34.2 per cent) said that the level of current business performance had not been affected in any discernible way. Almost none said that business performance was lower because of partnership. More than seven out of ten managers (71.6 per cent) said current workforce productivity was higher.

Less than a quarter (24.7 per cent) said there was no obvious effect while almost no managers said that workforce productivity was lower because of partnership.

There is, however, a striking difference between the reports on expected future outcomes and the reports on current outcomes. Managers clearly expected even more positive results from their partnership initiatives in the future than had been achieved to date. For example, almost nine out of ten managers (88.8 per cent) expected business performance to be higher as a result of partnership in the coming five years compared to about seven out of ten currently (64.4 per cent). Almost nine out of ten managers (87.7 per cent) also expected workforce productivity to be higher as a result of partnership in the coming five years compared to seven out of ten currently (71.6 per cent). In addition, the proportion of managers who considered that partnership would have no obvious effect on future business performance and workforce productivity was significantly reduced. Almost no one expected the partnership initiatives to have negative effects in the future on business performance or workforce productivity.

The findings were strongly positive, then, for current and future outcomes relating to business performance and workforce productivity. The most likely explanation for the difference between current and expected future outcomes is that these partnership initiatives were in many cases still at early stages of development and that the parties were handling issues and problems that would take more time to come to fruition. We saw earlier that it can take considerable time for managers, employees and union representatives to build up sufficient trust to enable them to expand their joint activities to encompass significant change agendas that, if handled successfully, might deliver important outcomes.

The Attitudes of Union Members

We have seen that one of the main objectives of innovative industrial relations and human resource practices for employers was to

deepen understanding among employees and trade union representatives of business issues and to encourage more flexible attitudes towards organisational change (Kochan and Osterman,
1994). We also saw that outcomes such as improved communications and higher trust can, in turn, impact on outcomes such as
business performance and workforce productivity (Cooke, 1990).
In Figure 6.2 we summarise the conclusions of managers on the
current and expected future outcomes of their partnership initiatives on union members' understanding of business issues, on
their support for change and on their flexibility in work practices.

Figure 6.2: Effects on Union Members' Attitudes

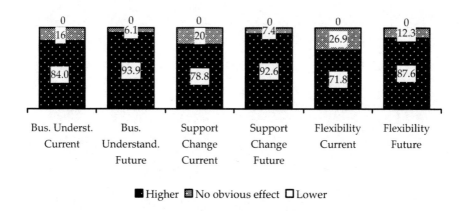

More than eight out of ten managers (84.0 per cent) reported
that current employee understanding of business issues was
higher due to the influence of partnership. Only 16.0 per cent said
that partnership had no obvious effect and there were no reports
of negative results. Almost eight out of ten respondents (78.8 per
cent) also reported that union members' current support for
change was higher. Twenty per cent said there had been no discernible effect while almost no one said it was lower. When asked
about changes in the current degree of employee flexibility in
work practices, about three quarters of the managers (71.8 per
cent) said that this was higher due to the influence of partnership.

A little more than a quarter (26.9 per cent) said partnership had made no obvious difference and almost no one reported negative results. These are also very positive results for the organisations concerned, particularly bearing in mind that most of the organisations had adversarial histories. Managers expected to achieve more in the future than had been achieved to date in regard to union members' attitudes towards change and flexibility.

Management Decision Making

We saw that risks for employers in adopting partnership included slower decision-making because of the need to inform and consult and ambiguity among employees regarding the right of managers to make decisions (Cooke, 1990; McKersie, 2002). The responses on these issues are summarised in Figure 6.3.

Figure 6.3: Effects on Speed of Decisions and Right to Decide

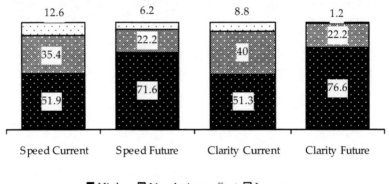

A little more than half of these managers (51.9 per cent) considered that the current speed of decision-making was higher in those parts of the organisation covered by partnership. A little more than a third (35.4 per cent) said that partnership had no obvious effect and a small minority (12.6 per cent) said that the current speed of decision-making was slower. When asked to what extent did they expect the speed of decision-making to be affected by partnership over the coming five years, almost three quarters (71.6 per cent) said they expected it to be higher. The numbers expecting partnership to have no obvious effect fell from 35.4 per cent to 22.2 per cent. Again, only a handful expected decision-making to be slower as a result of partnership.

A little more than half of the managers (51.3 per cent) also considered that current clarity on management's right to make decisions was higher. Four out of ten (40.0 per cent) considered that partnership had had no obvious effect on management's right to make decisions while almost no one (8.8 per cent) reported current negative effects. When asked about expected future outcomes, a little more than three quarters of managers (76.6 per cent) expected clarity re management's right to make decisions to be higher. Those expecting partnership to make no difference on this issue declined from 40.0 per cent to 22.2 per cent.

One of the assumptions behind partnership is that employee and trade union involvement can help to improve the quality of decision-making. In Figure 6.4 we summarise managers' perceptions on the effects of partnership on the quality of strategic and operational decisions currently and in the future.

Figure 6.4: Effects on Quality of Decision Making

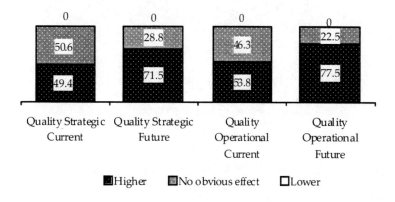

Almost half of all managers (49.4 per cent) considered that the current quality of strategic decisions was higher. Half (50.6 per cent) said that partnership had made no obvious difference. No one reported negative effects on strategic decisions. The numbers reporting improvements in operational decisions were similar. A little more than half (53.8 per cent) considered that the current quality of operational decisions was higher and a little less than half (46.3 per cent) said that partnership had made no obvious difference. No one reported negative effects on operational decisions.

Again, managers had higher expectations of the future effects of partnership on the quality of strategic and operational decisions. For example, 71.5 per cent of managers expected the quality of future strategic decisions to be higher compared to 49.4 per cent currently. Also, 77.5 per cent expected the quality of operational decisions to be higher in future compared to 53.8 per cent currently.

Another assumption behind partnership is that employees will develop a sense of ownership over decisions and that this will facilitate the implementation of workplace changes. Findings on the perceptions of managers on how partnership affects the implementation of decisions are summarised in Figure 6.5.

Figure 6.5: Effects on Implementation of Decision Making

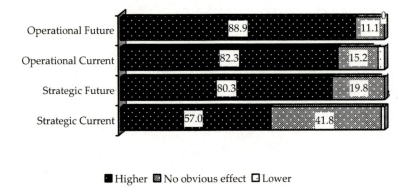

■ Higher ▨ No obvious effect ☐ Lower

Almost six out of ten managers (57.0 per cent) considered that the current effectiveness of implementation of strategic decisions was higher due to the influence of partnership. However, a considerable minority of 41.8 per cent said that partnership had made no obvious difference. Almost no one reported negative effects. The numbers reporting improvements in effectiveness of implementation of operational decisions were much higher. About eight out of ten managers (82.3 per cent) considered that the effectiveness of implementation of operational decisions was higher and 15.2 per cent said partnership had made no obvious difference. Managers also had higher expectations of the future effects of partnership on the effectiveness of implementation of strategic and operational decisions.

Overall, the findings on decision-making show that partnership delivers positive results. For example, not alone are there no negative effects such as ambiguity over management's right to make decisions or a slowing down of decision-making but the findings also indicate that there have been overall improvements in the quality of strategic and operational decision-making as well as in the effectiveness of implementation of decisions.

In sum, then, the overall results for employers appear strongly positive and to confirm the view that partnership can have positive overall outcomes that are likely to outweigh the costs concerned. On the other hand, the findings relating to future outcomes suggest that the full potential of partnership has not yet been realised.

Outcomes for Employees

The outcomes measured here were job satisfaction, security of employment, and pay and conditions. We have seen that one of the key assumptions behind partnership is that it can deliver 'mutual gains' or benefits to employees and trade unions as well as to employers. In Figure 6.6 we summarise how managers evaluated the current and future effects of partnership on employee job satisfaction, job security and pay and conditions of employment.

Slightly more than half of the managers responding (55.9 per cent) considered that current job satisfaction was higher in those parts of the organisation covered by partnership and about four out of ten (42.9 per cent) considered that partnership had no obvious effect. Almost no managers reported negative effects on job satisfaction. About half of those responding (44.7 per cent) said that current security of employment was higher as a result of partnership. A little more than half (48.7 per cent) said that partnership had no obvious effect on security of employment. A very small number (6.6 per cent) said that security of employment was slightly lower as a result of partnership. More than half of those responding (57.5 per cent) said that current levels of pay and conditions were higher due to partnership. A considerable minority of 42.5 per cent said partnership had no obvious effect. No one said that pay and conditions were worsened by partnership.

Figure 6.6: Effects on Job Satisfaction, Job Security and Pay

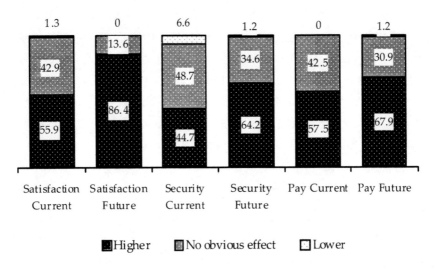

On the other hand, more respondents expected job satisfaction to be higher in the future as reported it higher currently (86.4 per cent as opposed to 55.9 per cent). The numbers expecting partnership to make no discernible difference to job satisfaction in the future fell from 42.9 per cent to 13.6 per cent. No respondents expected negative outcomes on job satisfaction concerned over the next five years.

More respondents expected security of employment to be higher in future because of partnership as reported it higher currently (64.2 per cent as opposed to 44.7 per cent). The numbers expecting partnership to make no difference to security of employment in the future fell from 48.7 per cent to 34.6 per cent. Almost no respondents expected negative outcomes for security of employment from partnership over the next five years.

Why, might it be that partnership appears to have a lesser positive impact on job security, which is a key outcome for employees and trade unions? The advocates of 'mutual gains' acknowledge the virtual impossibility of employers guaranteeing absolute job security and argue that a more realistic proposition would be for employers to give considerable weight to the jobs implications of major decisions, to first exhaust all the alternatives to layoffs and for the state to 'cushion' layoffs with training and other support programmes (Cooke, 1990; Kochan and Osterman, 1994). It appears to be the case, then, that competitive realities limit the potential that partnership has for delivering job security over the longer run.

Slightly more respondents (67.9 per cent) expected pay and conditions to be higher in future as a result of partnership as currently reported higher pay and conditions (57.5 per cent). The numbers expecting partnership to have no discernible effect on pay and conditions fell from 42.5 per cent to 30.9 per cent. There were almost no (1.2 per cent) expected negative outcomes as far as security of employment is concerned over the next five years.

In sum, then, as was the case with outcomes of particular importance to management, most respondents considered that partnership had positive outcomes for employees. They also considered that outcomes would be better in future than currently. However, it seems reasonable to conclude while partnership does have positive outcomes for employees this happens to a lesser extent than it does for management. This seems particularly true in respect to job security and pay and conditions. These findings appear to accord with the findings in the previous chapter that our respondents ranked agenda items of particular interest to employees lower in importance than agenda items of particular interest to management.

Outcomes for Trade Unions

We included two questions on outcomes we considered would be of particular importance for trade unions, viz the effects of partnership on management involvement of the union on a day-to-day basis and the effects of partnership on union influence on management decision making. Needless to say, the parties best positioned to comment on this question would be trade union representatives themselves and we outline in Appendix 1 why it was not possible to extend the survey to them.

We saw in the literature review that there was considerable controversy regarding the implications of partnership for trade unions (Kochan et al., 1984; Kelly, 2004; Clarke and Haiven, 1999; Bacon and Storey, 2000). One view suggested that unions could only survive and serve their members by embracing and shaping partnership; another view suggested that adversarial relationships could serve trade unions well and that partnership could be a recipe for marginalisation (Peetz, 1996). There was also an argument that union members wanted their unions to play both co-operative and adversarial roles at once, the former on issues such as work organisation and the latter on pay and conditions (Eaton et al., 1992; Geary, 2006).

In Figure 6.7 we set out the findings relating to current and future outcomes on the extent of management involvement of the union and on the extent of union influence.

Figure 6.7: Effects on Union Involvement and Influence

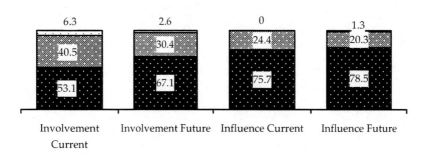

A little more than half of those responding (53.1 per cent) said that current management involvement of the union on a day-to-day basis was higher and four out of ten (40.5 per cent) said that partnership had no obvious effect on the current level of involvement. A small minority (6.3 per cent) reported that current management involvement of the union was lower as a result of partnership. Looking to the future, a slightly higher number of managers expected management involvement of unions to be higher (67.1 per cent as opposed to 53.1 per cent). Fewer managers (2.6 per cent as opposed to 6.3 per cent) expected partnership to lead to lower trade union involvement in the future.

About three-quarters of respondents (75.7 per cent) said that current union influence on management decision-making was higher as a result of partnership and 24.4 per cent said that partnership had no discernible effect. No one reported negative effects on union influence. A similar number of respondents expected union influence on management decision-making to be higher in the future (78.5 per cent and 75.7 per cent). There was no significant change in the numbers of those who thought that partnership would have no discernible effect on union influence (20.3 per cent in the future and 24.4 per cent currently). Almost no respondents (1.3 per cent) expected future negative effects on union influence.

Less than a quarter of managers (21.5 per cent) said that current staffing levels were higher as a result of partnership, see Figure 6.8. A majority (58.2 per cent) said that partnership had no obvious effect on current staffing levels. Less than a quarter (20.3 per cent) said that current staffing levels were lower. The majority of managers (63.0 per cent) considered that partnership would have no obvious effect on staffing levels over the next five years with 23.4 per cent considering that staffing levels would be higher as a result of partnership. The number of those who expected staffing levels to be lower was 13.6 per cent.

Figure 6.8: Effects on Staffing Levels

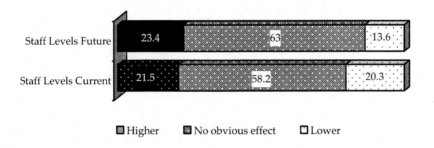

The findings suggest positive effects for trade unions as far as involvement and influence are concerned. On the other hand, partnership appears to have had little effect on staffing levels in the organisations concerned. Only a handful of respondents reported negative effects, thus lending no real support to the arguments of critics that partnership will lead to the weakening of union prerogatives and strength. On balance, it appears justified to conclude that partnership has positive outcomes for trade unions, again bearing in mind that the findings represent a management viewpoint.

Workplace Relationships Outcomes

We report here findings of value to all of the stakeholders, viz relationships outcomes such as the quality of communications, trust in the workplace, and management understanding of employee and trade union problems. Figure 6.9 summarises these findings.

More than eight out of ten respondents (86.3 per cent) said that the quality of current communications between managers and supervisors and employees and representatives was higher in those parts of the organisation covered by partnership. Only 13.8 per cent said that partnership had no discernible effect on communications and no respondents reported any negative effects.

Figure 6.9: Effects on Communications and Trust

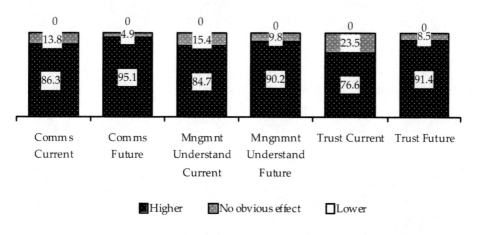

Slightly more respondents expected higher quality communications in the future as a result of partnership than reported this outcome currently (95.1 per cent compared to 86.3 per cent). The reports of no discernible effect fell from 13.8 per cent to 4.9 per cent.

More than eight out of ten respondents (84.7 per cent) reported that current management understanding of employee and trade union problems was higher as a result of partnership. Only 15.4 per cent said partnership had no discernible effect. No one reported negative effects. Slightly more respondents expected higher results over the coming five years in terms of management understanding of employee and trade union problems (90.2 per cent as opposed to 84.7 per cent). Less than one in ten (9.8 per cent) expected that partnership would have no discernible effect in the future. One manager wrote that partnership 'has created the climate within which better relationships between managers and staff are being evolved. Senior management have a much clearer perspective on the concerns and constituencies of unions and staff'.

Almost eight out of ten respondents (76.6 per cent) said that the current level of trust between managers/supervisors and employees/representatives was higher. Almost a quarter of respondents (23.5 per cent) said that partnership had no discernible effect on the level of trust but no respondents reported any negative effects. Slightly more respondents expected to see trust being higher in the future (91.4 per cent compared to 76.6 per cent). The incidence of no discernible effect fell from 23.5 per cent to 8.5 per cent.

In sum, the findings on current outcomes suggest quite positive effects for management-union-employee relationships in regard to communications, management understanding of employee and trade union problems and trust levels. The incidence of respondents saying that partnership has had no discernible effect ranges between 13.8 per cent and 23.5 per cent. At the same time it emerges, as it also did in respect to other outcomes, that there are higher expectations regarding the future as opposed to the current effects of partnership.

Industrial Relations Outcomes

Partnership is generally expected to lead to fewer industrial disputes. Figure 6.10 summarises the reports from managers in regard to industrial disputes and industrial relations grievances.

Figure 6.10: Effects on Industrial Disputes

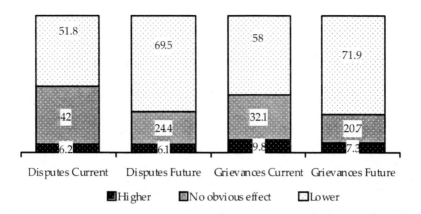

About half of all respondents (51.8 per cent) said that the current incidence of industrial disputes was lower in those parts of the organisation covered by partnership due to the influence of partnership. About four out of ten (42.0 per cent) said that partnership had no obvious effect while a very small proportion (6.2 per cent) said that the incidence of disputes was higher. More respondents expected that the level of disputes would be lower in the future than currently (69.5 per cent as opposed to 51.8 per cent). Those who expected partnership to have no obvious effect fell from 42.0 per cent to 24.4 per cent.

About half of all respondents (58.0 per cent) also said that the current incidence of industrial relations grievances from the workforce was lower. About a third (32.1 per cent) said that partnership had no obvious effect while a very small proportion (9.8 per cent) said that the incidence of grievances was higher. More respondents expected that the level of grievances would be lower in the future that currently (71.9 per cent as opposed to 58.0 per cent). Those who expected partnership to have no obvious effect on the incidence of grievances in the future also fell.

We don't know what the incidence of disputes and grievances was in these organisations prior to their partnership initiatives. Nevertheless, these reports from managers are strongly positive as far as the effects of partnership on industrial relations disputes and grievances are concerned. It is worth bearing in mind that management and trade unions commonly attempt to resolve out- standing differences as part of their preparations for developing partnership and that this might lead to a reduced number of is- sues in dispute in the early days of partnership. This can some- times have negative effects, however, as instanced by one man- ager who commented that 'when we tried to introduce partner- ship as part of the national agreement we were met with demands to resolve all outstanding issues before the unions would partici- pate. We found this difficult as it was hardly partnership where one side was expected to pay for change up-front'. Another man- ager commented that 'partnership has brought about many im- provements and the most noticeable is the improved industrial relations environment'.

We have already seen that the relationship between existing collective bargaining systems and new partnership arrangements could provide sources of tension. We saw, for example, that col- lective bargaining issues were usually excluded from the partner- ship agenda, at least in the early stages (HRDC, 1998). We also saw that both management and unions sought to influence the distribution of issues between collective bargaining and partner- ship (Marks et al., 1998; Bacon and Storey, 2000).

In Figure 6.11 we report on the effects of partnership on the collective bargaining agenda.

More than a third of managers (37.8 per cent) said the collec- tive bargaining agenda was the same, more than a quarter (28.0 per cent) said there were more issues on the agenda and slightly more than a third (34.2 per cent) also said there were fewer issues on the agenda. These findings suggest quite different experiences of partnership among respondents and they are difficult to inter- pret. That slightly more than a third of respondents report the agenda being the same is not surprising given that there will inevitably be a continuing collective bargaining agenda in most organisations that adopt partnership.

Figure 6.11: Effects on Content of Collective Bargaining Agenda

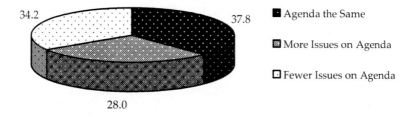

A little more than a quarter of respondents saying that there are more issues on the agenda may be considered two ways: it may indicate increased adversarialism (other findings do not appear to support such a reading) or it may indicate that the partnership process has opened up issues that have an industrial relations dimension and that having more issues on the agenda may be considered a positive development from both managerial and trade union perspectives. Finally, one third of respondents reporting fewer issues on the agenda may indicate the settlement of outstanding issues as part of the establishment of partnership or the transfer of certain issues from collective bargaining into partnership. It will be seen below that about a third of respondents said that major issues that had previously been decided by management and unions together through collective bargaining had been passed into partnership.

We report in Figure 6.12 findings relating to the movement of issues from the collective bargaining agenda to partnership.

When asked had issues that were previously handled through collective bargaining been passed into the partnership system, more than a quarter of those responding (28.4 per cent) said that they had not. More than a third (40.7 per cent) said that minor issues had been transferred and slightly less than a third (30.9 per cent) said that major issues had been transferred from collective bargaining to partnership.

Figure 6.12: Passing Issues from Collective Bargaining to Partnership

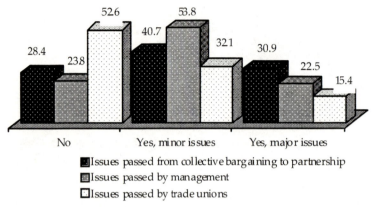

When asked had issues that were previously decided solely by management (separate from collective bargaining) been passed into partnership less than a quarter (23.8 per cent) said that they had not. More than half (53.8 per cent) said that minor issues had been passed into the partnership system and less than a quarter (22.5 per cent) said that major issues had been transferred.

Finally, when asked had the unions put issues into the partnership system such as demarcation and staffing levels that in the past were handled through collective bargaining, more than half (52.6 per cent) said that they had not. About a third (32.1 per cent) only 15.4 per cent said they had put major issues into partnership.

When asked was collective bargaining more or less adversarial as a consequence of partnership, only a small minority of those responding (4.9 per cent) said that it was more adversarial, the majority (66.7 per cent) said it was less adversarial and 28.4 per cent said it was just the same. See Figure 6.13.

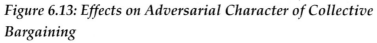

Figure 6.13: Effects on Adversarial Character of Collective Bargaining

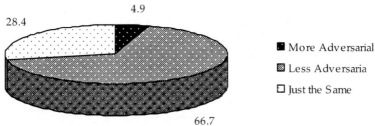

When asked had the effectiveness of collective bargaining been improved by partnership, 18.5 per cent said it was significantly improved, 56.8 per cent said it was improved somewhat, and 24.7 percent said it was just the same. When asked if issues that in the past were handled through collective bargaining and that were now handled through partnership had to be ratified through collective bargaining, 18.4 per cent said 'yes, always', 64.5 per cent said 'yes, sometimes' and 17.1 per cent said 'no, not at all'.

These findings suggest that partnership has positive effects for management and trade unions in one of their most important institutions, viz the collective bargaining process. There appears to be a greater degree of caution on the part of the trade unions as far as the transfer of issues into partnership is concerned. At the same time, respondents indicated that in almost a half of all cases the unions had transferred either minor or major issues into the partnership process.

In Exhibit 6.1 we give a brief description of how traditional industrial relations issues such as staff transfers, pensions and pay can be handled through partnership. AXA Insurance is a general insurance company with 1000 employees (Cummins, 2009). About 75 per cent of AXA employees are members of either SIPTU or UNITE. In some cases issues might be handled entirely through partnership. In other cases, issues might be raised through partnership and then handled through formal industrial relations channels but with the benefit of the positive 'spill over' effects from an effective partnership into the collective bargaining arena.

Exhibit 6.1 AXA Insurance

AXA Insurance had a history of adversarial industrial relations with SIPTU and UNITE. The parties developed a partnership approach to organisational change to help improve relationships. Partnership in AXA is structured around local forums including a 'claims forum', a 'customer service centre forum' and a 'branch network forum'. Having these local forums gave management opportunities to engage positively with staff and resolve local issues that were causing difficulties. The company's experience of resistance to change initiatives was that this often happened, not because significant changes were unacceptable, but because smaller issues had not been addressed. Senior participants from these local groups are represented on a higher level 'employer of choice forum' which handles companywide or strategic issues such as pensions, moving 150 jobs from Dublin to Derry, and terms and conditions of employment. Through structured consultation, management and unions developed a higher level of mutual trust and the unions developed a stronger appreciation of the business environment. In recent years, the company took the view that its remuneration system was not sustainable. Revenues were falling, costs were increasing, and the historical pay structures meant that pay rates were increasing at a pace that was out of line with other parts of the company. Management raised the issue through the 'employer of choice forum' in late 2007. The company issued proposals to the unions in early 2008 and with the help of an agreed mediator, agreement was reached in mid-2008. The new arrangements provided for pay movements being tied to national programme increases only (or a locally agreed rate in event of no national agreement), salary band limits being reduced by 15 to 20 per cent, a reduction in the number of higher earners by at least 100. The company also agreed to an additional salary review process for employees under €30,000.

Management and Trade Union Support for Partnership

We have seen already that strong commitment by all parties, particularly management and trade union leaders, is essential to the longer term success of partnership initiatives (Cooke, 1990; Kochan and Dyer, 1976; Cohen-Rosenthal and Burton, 1987; Woodworth and Meek, 1994; HRDC, 1998). In Figure 6.14 we report the findings relating to changes in levels of support for partnership as currently reported and as expected in the future.

Figure 6.14: Effects on Support for Partnership

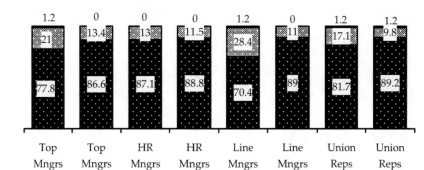

More than three quarters of those responding (77.8 per cent) said the degree of support for partnership was now higher among top managers. Slightly more expected higher support for partnership among top managers in future (86.6 per cent as compared to 77.8 per cent). More than eight out of ten respondents (87.1 per cent) said the degree of support for partnership was higher among HR managers. Slightly more respondents expected higher support for partnership among HR managers in future as reported currently (88.8 per cent as compared to 86.6 per cent). Seven out of ten line managers (70.4 per cent) were also said to have a higher degree of support.

Almost nine out of ten respondents (89.0 per cent) expected the level of support for partnership among line managers to be higher compared to 70.4 per cent currently. More than eight out of ten respondents (81.7 per cent) said the level of support for partnership was higher among shop stewards. Slightly more expected this level of support to be even higher in future (89.2 per cent as compared to 81.7 per cent).

Almost no one reported that the degree of support for partnership had declined among any of these groups and the figures for making no discernible difference were 21.0 per cent among top managers, 13.0 per cent among HR managers, 28.4 per cent – the highest figure – among line managers, and 17.1 per cent – the lowest figure – among shop stewards.

In sum, then, the findings suggest that the groups that have the highest levels of support for partnership arising from partnership are HR managers and shop stewards. This is perhaps not surprising given that these groups might be expected on the one hand to be the most involved in partnership and on the other hand to have the most to gain in terms of improved relationships and reduced incidence of disputes and grievances.

Discussion of Findings on Outcomes

Other research supports the view that partnership has positive outcomes for employers in Ireland, for example in respect to costs, competitiveness, production processes, product quality, and effort to get the job done (Totterdill and Sharpe, 1999:47-64: NCPP, 2002; Roche, 2009). There is also evidence of positive relationships outcomes such as greater employee understanding of customer needs, improved communications and trust; a better appreciation of how to manage change; reduced conflict; better mutual understanding between management and trade unions; more effective use of collective bargaining; a reduced use of third parties to resolve disputes; and increased organisational commitment (Healy.

2000:17; NCPP, 2002; Roche, 2009). Partnership allows companies to harness the tacit knowledge and innovative potential of the workforce (Totterdill and Sharpe, 1999; O'Donnell and Teague, 2000).

On the other hand, Hastings (2003) shows in the case of Aer Lingus that many senior managers considered partnership too slow, too amenable to union influence, not sufficiently amenable to management unilateralism, and less effective as a means of implementing changes than a combination of industrial relations and direct employee involvement.

Positive outcomes for employees that have been identified in other Irish research include: greater confidence and self-esteem, greater insights into business problems, more control over work leading to increased job satisfaction, a say in workplace organisation and some influence over business decisions, influence over strategic business decisions, more time for family life arising from annualised hours and elimination of overtime, employee share ownership, and a better quality of working life (Totterdill and Sharpe, 1999: 47-64; NCPP, 2002; Hastings, 2003).

Other research also finds that 'partnership practices and arrangements' in unionised companies are positively associated with employee outcomes such as 'intrinsic' aspects of work including work autonomy, the provision of information, job satisfaction and perceptions of fairness (Roche, 2006). Neither work intensity nor levels of work-related stress were affected either way by partnership and there were no positive associations between partnership and 'extrinsic' aspects of work such as employment security or earnings (Roche, 2006).

There is some evidence of stabilised industrial relations and improved organisational performance leading to better security of employment and enhanced terms and conditions (NCPP, 2002). Nevertheless a majority of employees taking part in the review of the *IPC New Work Organization Programme* said that they had not yet seen significant gains and many were sceptical about whether partnership would be advantageous to them personally (Totterdill and Sharpe, 1999: 47-64). There is also some evidence that the process benefits of partnership, the access to information and ideas etc. brought benefits to a select group of workers and managers and not to the entire workforce (O'Donnell and Teague, 2000: 25). It seems that the more that employees are directly involved with partnership the more positive their perceptions of the company and the more committed they are to the partnership process (Totterdill and Sharpe, 1999: 47-64).

There is little available evidence on the outcomes of partnership for trade unions in Ireland. Roche (2009) concluded that partnership has net overall positive outcomes for unions. He found that positive net gains appeared to arise for unions in regard to union commitment, union influence and the likelihood of union membership. However, it appeared that membership commitment to the union decreased as commitment to the company increased. Roche also concluded that partnership practices and arrangements seemed to influence outcomes for employers and trade unions indirectly and not directly, i.e. mainly through their effects on employee attitudes and behaviour (Roche, 2009).

On the basis of our own findings and on the findings of others it seems reasonable to conclude that partnership overall has positive outcomes for management, employees and trade unions but to a somewhat greater extent for management.

Summary and Conclusions

In this chapter we provided the most detailed account to date of conclusions that senior managers in Ireland have come to on the outcomes of partnership initiatives in their organisations. The findings showed positive outcomes for employers, employees and trade unions with no negative effects. At the same time there appeared to be limited benefits for employees in respect to key outcomes such as job security and staffing levels. In terms of 'mutual gains' it appeared that more benefits were accruing to management than to employees. Finally, there was a striking difference in the findings for current and expected future outcomes. Respondents had higher expectations of partnership over future years and considered that the maximum benefits of partnership had not yet been realised.

In the next chapter we explore whether or not different sets of circumstances give rise to different types of partnership and whether different types have different outcomes.

7

PARTNERSHIP TYPES: INFLUENCES AND OUTCOMES

In the previous chapters we explored the factors that gave rise to partnership, how partnerships operated in terms of structures and agendas, and what outcomes they produced for management, employees and trade unions. We now turn our attention to how we might classify cases into different types of partnership. There are two main reasons why we want to investigate partnership types. Firstly, we want to explore whether or not different sets of circumstances might lead to the emergence of different types of partnership. Secondly, we want to explore whether or not some types of partnership lead to better outcomes and, indeed, 'mutual gains' for employers, employees and trade unions and, if so, what types? Answering these questions is not just an academic exercise: if we can identify factors that are likely to lead to partnerships that have substantial benefits for employers, trade unions and employees then we can suggest how employers and trade unions might design and develop partnerships so as to increase the likelihood of substantial outcomes for all stakeholders. This is also an important issue for policy makers and support agencies in the fields of industrial relations and industrial development. This is a largely unexplored aspect of workplace partnership both internationally and in Ireland. We are, therefore, taking a tentative and exploratory approach to the elaboration of partnership types.

Categorising Partnerships into Different Types

We saw in Chapter 3 that workplace partnerships have structures that are separate from collective bargaining arrangements. We also saw that, at least initially, partnership agendas are intended to be different to collective bargaining agendas. Researchers have sought to explain how partnership leads to positive outcomes by examining the effects of partnership structures and agendas. Not surprisingly, then, researchers have also used structures and agendas as ways of categorising partnership cases into different types. There is, however, no agreed way of doing this.

Nevertheless, based on our reading of the international and Irish literatures, we have chosen to construct our classification of types around partnership structures and agendas. Structures are the formal bodies such as committees and forums that management and trade unions put in place following their decisions to establish partnership. Agendas are the issues and problems that the parties agree to work on through these bodies.

We saw from the international research that there was a strong argument that partnerships that had both strategic and operational bodies were more likely to generate significant outcomes than partnerships that had only strategic or partnership bodies. We also saw in chapter five that our strategic and operational bodies involved management and union representatives as well as individual employees. In the literature there was also a strong argument that it was more beneficial in terms of outcomes to have a mix of representative and direct forms. On this basis, we distinguished between structures that were 'limited', i.e. having strategic or operational partnership bodies only and that were 'extensive', i.e. having both strategic and operational bodies.

We distinguished between agendas that were 'weighty' or 'light' in the volume of 'hard' and 'soft' 'mainstream' agenda items they addressed including issues such as such as changes in work practices, new technology, changes in pay systems, information around company plans and strategies, improving communications etc. (NCPP, 2003: 12). Thus we arrived at four partnership types as illustrated in Table 7.1.

Table 7.1: Four Partnership Types

	Partnership Type 1 – 'Exploratory'	Partnership Type 2 – 'Integrated Exploratory'	Partnership Type 3 – 'Business'	Partnership Type 4 – 'Integrated Business'
Number of Cases	31	32	6	10
Main Features	A light mainstream agenda with strategic or operational bodies only	A light mainstream agenda with both strategic and operational bodies	A weighty mainstream agenda with strategic or operational bodies only	A weighty mainstream agenda with both strategic and operational bodies

We used the answers to our yes/no questions relating to the presence of strategic and operational partnership bodies to separate out cases based on structures. We defined 'weighty' agendas as those that respondents identified as having two-thirds or more of whichever agenda applied; all others were considered to be 'light'.[1]

The first type, which we call 'exploratory', has a light mainstream agenda with a limited number of mainstream issues and a limited structure, i.e. either strategic or operational partnership bodies but not both. The second type, which we call 'integrated exploratory', has a light mainstream agenda but it has extensive structures, i.e. both strategic and operational bodies. The third type, which we call 'business', has a weighty mainstream agenda and either strategic or operational partnership structures but not

---

[1] See Appendix for details on the operationalisation of the four types.

both. The term 'business' is intended to convey the greater weight in the partnership agendas in this type and not simply a concentration on issues that might be considered more important to employers than to employees and trade unions.

The fourth type, which we call 'integrated business', has a weighty mainstream agenda and it has both strategic and operational structures. Within the international literature exploratory and integrated exploratory types would be considered as 'weak' forms of partnership while the two business types would be considered as 'strong'.

When we operationalised the four types, 31 emerged as exploratory cases, 23 with operational bodies only and eight with strategic bodies only. There were 32 integrated exploratory partnerships. There were six business partnerships, five with operational bodies only and one with strategic bodies only. There were ten integrated business partnerships. It should be noted that categorising cases in this way is based on a simple 'snapshot' in time rather than a detailed analysis over time. It is not to suggest that cases remain static and locked into any one type. Clearly they can evolve and develop as well as regress and weaken over time.

Exploring Influences on the Development of Partnership Types

In this section we explore the external and internal factors influencing the development of our partnership types on which we gathered data in the survey. In essence, our concern here is to answer the following question: given the levels of risk for management and trade unions in deciding to handle workplace issues affecting management and staff in an untested partnership process, why are some organisations that adopt workplace partnership more likely than others to develop one type as opposed to another? We are assuming that certain sets of external business factors such as serious commercial difficulties and certain internal organisational factors such as the quality of management-union relationships would influence the types of partnerships that employers and trade unions would develop. We are also assuming that it is more likely that influences will work in configurations of multiple influences than separately as individual influences.

We are suggesting that exploratory and integrated exploratory partnerships are likely to develop in similar circumstances to each other and that business and integrated business partnership types are also likely to develop in similar circumstances to each other. Our available theories and knowledge of partnership do not provide a foundation that is solid enough on which to conjecture that completely different sets of circumstances are likely to be associated with each of the four partnership types (Cooke, 1990; Kelly; 2004). The partnerships we are researching are, in effect, new phenomena for researchers as well as for practitioners within the industrial relations field and, as one commentator has observed, our understanding of partnership remains highly fragmented and incomplete (Cooke, 1990).

On this basis, then, when we are exploring the possible links between different sets of circumstances and partnership types we will reduce the four types to two – an 'exploratory' type that encompasses both 'exploratory' and 'integrated exploratory' partnerships and a 'business' type that encompasses both 'business' and 'integrated business' types. What separates these exploratory (i.e. exploratory and integrated exploratory combined) and business partnerships (i.e. business and integrated business combined) is their agendas, 'light' in the volume of 'hard' and 'soft' 'mainstream' agenda items in the case of exploratory partnership and 'weighty' in the volume of 'hard' and 'soft' 'mainstream' agenda items in the case of business partnerships.

In addition, we need to express caution on the numbers of cases available for exploring influences on the development of types. We have reduced our sample from 88 cases to 79 because of inadequate responses on some of the key variables relating to structures and agendas. Also, we only have six business partnerships. These low numbers render problematical some of the statistical analysis and require us to be very tentative around certain conclusions arising from this analysis.

We are, however, suggesting that there will be differences in outcomes between the four partnership types. Consequently, when we are exploring the possible links between partnership types and outcomes we will extend the exploration to all four types.

Table 7.2 summarises the assumptions we are making about the types of factors likely to influence the development of exploratory and business partnerships.

Table 7.2: Circumstances Influencing Exploratory and Business Partnerships

Exploratory Partnerships (Exploratory and Integrated Exploratory Types Combined)	**Business Partnerships** (Business and Integrated Business Types Combined)
Circumstances Likely to Lead to Exploratory Partnerships	*Circumstances Likely to Lead to Business Partnership*
• Anticipated significant future changes cited as important reason for adopting partnership	• Serious commercial difficulties cited as important reason for adopting partnership
• Experimenting with partnership cited as important reason for adopting partnership	• Anticipated need for further investment cited as important reason for adopting partnership
• Serious commercial difficulties not cited as important reason for adopting partnership	• Very poor relationships with unions and workforce not cited as important reason for adopting partnership
• Anticipated need for further investment not cited as important reason for adopting partnership	• High degree of trade union involvement on a day-to-day basis
• Very poor relationships with unions and workforce cited as important reason for adopting partnership	• High level of support for partnership among top management

• Less than high degree of trade union involvement on a day-to-day basis	• High level of support for partnership among full-time union officials
• Less than high level of support for partnership among top management	• Experimenting with partnership not cited as important reason for adopting partnership
• Less than high level of support for partnership among full-time union officials	• Anticipated significant future changes not cited as important reason for adopting partnership

Our argument relating to exploratory partnerships with their light agendas is that these are more likely to develop where there are weak external and internal pressures on organisations to carry the risks associated with partnership. So, we are assuming that in such cases the reasons that will be cited as important for adopting partnership will be anticipated significant future changes, experimenting with partnership, and very poor relationships with unions and workforce. We are assuming that serious commercial difficulties and the need for further investment will not be cited as important reasons for adopting partnership. We are also assuming that organisations that develop exploratory partnerships will not have high degrees of trade union involvement on a day-to-day basis or high levels of support for partnership among top management and full-time union officials. In sum, we are assuming that this set of circumstances or combination of influences would only be conducive to the development of a light partnership agenda, i.e. one that would carry few risks for management and trade unions in an untested partnership process.

Our argument relating to business partnerships with their weighty agendas is that these are more likely to develop where there are strong external and internal pressures on organisations to carry the risks associated with partnership. So, we are assuming that in such cases the reasons that will be cited as important for adopting partnership will be serious commercial difficulties and the need for further investment. We are assuming that very poor relationships, anticipation of significant future changes and experimenting with partnership will not be cited as important reasons for adopting partnership. We are assuming that there will be high degrees of trade union involvement on a day-to-day basis as well as high levels of support for partnership among top management and full-time union officials.

Because there are also high levels of trade union involvement and, implicitly, high levels of trade union membership, management will not have the facility to introduce changes unilaterally and must devise effective ways of involving unions, separate from traditional collective bargaining. Even then, where such pressures exist, we are suggesting that for management and unions to agree to tackle weighty agendas they will need to have high quality relationships and a high degree of support for the partnership initiative from senior management and full-time union officials. Absent a set of factors such as these it is difficult to envisage management and unions running the risks associated with business partnerships.

We next explore these lines of argument in two steps using cluster analysis. Firstly, we seek to establish whether influences on organisations adopting partnership form distinct clusters or configurations and, if so, what the features of these clusters are. Secondly, we consider whether any pattern of association between these clusters and our partnership types emerges from the analysis.[2]

Findings on Influences on Partnership Types

Table 7.3 shows how the factors that we assumed would have the most influence on the development of our exploratory and business partnership types clustered together in two configurations. The detailed cluster table is in Appendix 1.

---

[2] Cluster analysis is the appropriate statistical approach in this situation; see Appendix.

Table 7.3: Two Configurations of Circumstances Based on Reasons for Adopting Partnership and IR Characteristics

Variables	Cluster 1 – 'Continuous Change and Very Poor Relationships'	Cluster 2 – 'Future Changes and Experimentation'
Serious commercial difficulties necessitated significant changes for which we required the support of the workforce	Very Important	Of Some Little Importance
Very poor relationships with unions and workforce and we wanted to find ways of improving them	Important	Of Some Little Importance
Anticipated significant future changes in our commercial situation and we wanted to prepare the organisation for this	Very Important	Important
Anticipated the need for further investment and could only obtain this on basis of major changes in management-union relations and work practices	Very Important	Of Some Little Importance
Experimenting with partnership to see what benefits it might bring	Of Some Little Importance	Important
Degree of trade union involvement on a day-to-day basis	Moderate	Low
Level of support for partnership among top management	High	High
Level of support for partnership among full-time union officials	High	High

The organisations in Cluster 1 cited serious commercial difficulties and the need for further investment as important reasons for adopting partnership. They also cited very poor relationships and anticipated future change as important reasons. Experimenting with partnership was not an important reason for adopting partnership. The organisations in this cluster had a moderate degree of trade union involvement and high levels of support for partnership among top management and full-time union officials. In sum, this cluster represents a set of circumstances characterized by strong external and internal pressures for change that suggest a 'turbulent' external environment combined with a need to improve relationships within the organisation. On this basis, we are terming Cluster 1 'continuous change and very poor relationships' to capture the distinguishing characteristics of the organisations in this cluster, i.e. the presence of strong imperatives for immediate *and* future change arising from serious commercial difficulties *and* very poor relationships between management, unions and workforce.

The organisations in Cluster 2 cited anticipated significant future changes and experimenting with partnership as important reasons for adopting partnership. They cited serious commercial pressures *and* very poor relationships *and* the need for further investment as of some *little* importance in the adoption of partnership. The organisations in this cluster had a low degree of trade union involvement and high levels of support for partnership among top management and full-time union officials. In sum, this cluster represents a set of circumstances, characterised by relatively weak external pressures for change and little need to improve internal relationships, that suggest a 'calm' external environment combined with a small need to improve relationships. On this basis, we are terming Cluster 2 'future changes and experimentation' to capture the distinguishing characteristics of the organisations in this cluster, i.e. the *absence* of the kinds of strong imperatives for immediate and future change that characterised our 'continuous change and very poor relationships' cluster.

To what extent, then, do these clusters confirm our assumptions about the types of circumstances likely to influence the development of our exploratory and business partnerships? There appears to be a good degree of correspondence in respect to external influences between the two clusters and the two sets of circumstances that we had conjectured would influence the development of our two types. Organisations in the 'turbulent' 'continuous change and very poor relationships' cluster certainly feature stronger external pressures than organisations in the 'calm' 'future changes and experimentation' cluster.

There is not, however, a similar degree of correspondence in respect to internal influences between the two clusters and the two sets of circumstances that we had conjectured would influence the development of our two partnership types. While there is some small difference between the clusters in terms of levels of trade union involvement on a day-to-day basis there is no difference when it comes to levels of support for partnership among senior managers and trade union representatives.

It does, however, appear that there is a sufficient degree of correspondence between the clusters and the two sets of circumstances that we had conjectured would influence the development of our two partnership types for us to proceed to the second step in the analysis. The second step is to see if our exploratory types are more likely to appear in the 'calm' cluster and if our business types are more likely to appear in the 'turbulent' cluster.

Table 7.4 shows the distribution of our partnership types in the two clusters. More than eight out of ten of the business partnerships (85.7 per cent) appear in the 'turbulent' 'continuous change and very poor relationships' cluster. However, a little more than half of the exploratory partnerships (51.9 per cent) also appear in this cluster.

The findings broadly accord with our conjecture that business partnerships will be more strongly associated with 'turbulent' influences. They provide some support that exploratory partnerships will be associated with 'calm' influences albeit, as seen here, that slightly more of the exploratory cases (51.9 per cent) appear in the 'turbulent' cluster than appear in the 'calm' cluster (48.1 per cent). In sum, it seems reasonable to state that different sets of influences do cluster into two distinct configurations of 'turbulent' and 'calm' external and internal influences but in some important respects in a different way to what we had conjectured. It may not be surprising that the findings are not more clear-cut given the complexity of the phenomena under study and the exploratory nature of the research. Nevertheless we have to take up the challenge of explaining these findings.

Table 7.4: The Two Partnership Types and the Two Clusters Cross-tabulated

	'Continuous Change and Poor Relationships' Cluster	'Future Changes and Experimentation' Cluster
Business Partnerships	85.7%	14.3%
Exploratory Partnerships	51.9%	48.1%

One line of explanation for why the clusters did not correspond more precisely with the two sets of circumstances that we assumed would influence the development of our two partnership types might relate to how we interpret the cluster findings. As already seen above, we had conjectured that the two clusters would feature different strong influences and that there would be little similarity between them. However, it emerged that the two clusters differed, in the main, more in the degree to which certain factors such as serious commercial difficulties, anticipated future changes and very poor relationships were rated as important in the decision to adopt partnership. It might make more sense, then, to think of the external and internal circumstances influencing the development of our two types as two ends of a continuum as opposed to two mutually exclusive 'boxes'. Some organisations, for example, may have very strong external pressures combined with very poor internal relationships while other organisations may have less strong external pressures but still have very poor internal relationships.

Another line of explanation might relate to our assumptions about the importance of good relationships for the emergence of business partnerships. We had assumed that very poor relationships would be more strongly associated with exploratory than with business partnerships. The cluster analysis did not support this assumption. It is worth noting that the international literature shows that strong relationships (Heckscher, 1988; Rubinstein and Kochan, 2000) and very poor relationships (Cutcher-Gershenfeld and Verma, 1994; Kochan and Dyer, 1976) may both be associated with partnership. A relationships crisis, we saw in Chapter 3, can serve to 'get the attention' of management, unions and workers and to focus their attention on the need for improvement. We also know that most companies that took part in the EU-funded partnership projects in Ireland had a strong 'them and us' culture typified by low employee trust in management and an adversarial industrial relations history and climate (Totterdill and Sharpe, 1999; Healy, 2000). A number of these companies took part in the survey. We may, therefore, have given too much weight to the importance of previous good relationships as a factor likely to strongly influence the development of one type of partnership as opposed to another.

A possible explanation for why about half of our exploratory cases appear in the 'turbulent' empirical cluster might be found in the 'process' aspects of partnership. In other words, the explanation for why some cases developed into business types while others remained exploratory might be found in the ways in which management and trade unions handled these process aspects, in particular training and facilitation and senior management and trade union leadership.

We saw in Chapter 3 that developing and sustaining partnership over time and 'institutionalising' it as day-to-day practice are a major challenge for employers and trade unions (Kochan and

Dyer, 1976; Kochan et al., 1984). McAdam (1999), for example, describes the development of partnership in Aer Lingus as a very demanding process that requires a good deal of risk taking and leadership on the part of managers, union representatives and staff as well as major initiatives in communications, training and development. The social partners in *Partnership 2000* acknowledged that for some employers, employees, and their representatives, the move to a partnership culture would require a radical change in current attitudes and approaches (Government of Ireland, 1997).

We also saw that training in joint problem solving, interest-based bargaining, consensus decision-making, and conflict resolution can be helpful in the development of partnership. The experience in Ireland appears to bear this out (SIPTU, 2000). We saw in Chapter 5 that a majority of participants in the partnership bodies covered by this research received training but that joint training was provided in less than half of cases. Significant minorities received no training at all.

Another important 'process' aspect of partnership is having skilled and independent third-party consultants and facilitators who can help to shore up relationships weaknesses during the early phases of the development of partnership (Bushe, 1988; Cohen, Rosenthal and Burton, 1987). We saw in Chapter 5 that most of our partnership bodies did not use facilitators at their meetings.

Top executives and union leaders can significantly help overcome such difficulties where they show strong leadership in the development of partnership (Kochan and Dyer, 1976; Cohen-Rosenthal and Burton, 1987; Woodworth and Meek, 1994; HRDC, 1998). But there are also successful cases where such strong leadership is not present before partnership is developed (Bushe, 1988). Research suggests that management support can be as much an outcome as an input with managers becoming convinced to accept more union involvement as they see performance and relationships improvements arising from partnership (Clarke and Haiven, 1999).

It is possible, therefore, that the presence of skilful and committed leaders on both management and union sides and the provision of effective training and facilitation supports may have made the difference in terms of some organisations developing business partnerships while others developed exploratory ones in the same set of circumstances. Such leadership may also explain why some business partnerships developed against a background of apparently weak influences, i.e. the 14.3 per cent of business partnership cases that appear in our 'future changes and experimentation' cluster.

Indeed, cases such as Eircom and Aer Rianta highlight how the development of partnership around anticipated future changes as opposed to an immediate and pressing crisis can lead to the development of partnerships with weighty agendas (Hastings, 2003; Roche and Geary, 2006). In these cases not alone was there strong leadership on both management and union sides but certain of the key leaders had close and positive working relationships with each other and they acted in concert as well as separately as sponsors and trouble-shooters in the development of their partnerships. We know that extensive training and facilitation was also important in these cases (Hastings, 2003; Roche and Geary, 2006). While we included questions on training and facilitation in the survey, these questions were not of such detail as to provide fertile grounds for assessing their contribution to the development of partnership types. We did not include questions on leadership because we considered it too difficult to measure within such a broad survey.

Finally, we need to consider the possibility that the development of different types of partnership cannot be explained using simple models such as those we have applied. It might be that this can only be explained by a more complex interplay of factors that have not to date been described or understood to date in the research literature (Roche et al., 1998). At the end of the day, it is clear that the forces that determine whether one partnership will be an exploratory as opposed to a business type, as we have defined them here, are more complex than hitherto understood and more difficult, therefore, to model in research.

Exploring the Effects of Partnership Types on Outcomes

We now turn to the exploration of the four partnership types and their impact on outcomes. We are conjecturing that our 'strong' types ('business' and 'integrated business') will yield more significant outcomes than our 'weak' types ('exploratory' and 'integrated exploratory'). Our conjecture that the 'strong' types would have more significant outcomes than the 'weak' types is based on two assumptions. The first assumption is that more significant outcomes will ensue where management and unions are handling a weighty number of significant 'mainstream' issues, i.e. that the volume or weight of the agenda matters. The second assumption is that more significant outcomes will ensue where there are both operational and strategic partnership bodies. We have seen that operational bodies provide for engagement between managers, employees and union representatives at 'shop floor' level around operational issues of concern to them. We have seen that strategic bodies, involving as they do top management and union officials, have greater potential than bodies of an operational type to gain the support of managers, employees and union representatives. In sum, we have also seen that the combination of operational and strategic bodies provides scope for more extensive engagement between management, employees and union representatives at different levels of organisation, i.e. the structures matter as well as the agendas.

We expect that exploratory partnerships will have lesser outcomes than the other partnership types because of the light character of the agenda and the limited nature of the partnership structures. We expect that integrated exploratory partnerships will have stronger outcomes than exploratory cases because of their more extensive structures. We expect that business partnerships will have greater outcomes than exploratory or integrated exploratory partnerships because of their weighty agendas. Finally, we expect that integrated business partnerships will have the greatest impact of the four types on outcomes because they have more extensive structures and a weighty agenda. We are also interested in seeing if the achievement of 'mutual gains' outcomes is influenced by partnership types (Kochan and Osterman, 1994; Guest and Peccei, 2001; Knell, 1999).

Current Outcomes for Management, Employees and Trade Unions

In order to explore relationships between the four types of partnership and their outcomes we used a statistical technique called 'regression analysis'.[3] Table 7.5 sets out the standardised beta coefficients for our partnership types and the dependent variables for the current outcomes likely to be of specific importance to management, employees and trade unions.

Partnership type appears to have a significant effect on all the outcomes variables of importance to management, i.e. business performance, workforce productivity, union members' attitudes around business issues, support for change and flexibility in work practices, and how partnership affects the quality of operational and strategic decisions and their implementation. The table suggests that both integrated exploratory and integrated business partnerships have broadly equivalent positive effects for these management outcomes and stronger effects than either business or exploratory partnerships. In only two instances – union members' understanding of business issues and clarity re management's right to manage – does the business partnership type ap-

---

[3] See Appendix.

pear to have more positive effects than the exploratory and integrated exploratory types.

Table 7.5: Partnership Types and Current Outcomes

Dependent Variables	Standardised Beta Coefficients		
	Integrated Exploratory Partnerships	*Business Partnerships*	*Integrated Business Partnerships*
Outcomes of Importance to Management			
Business performance	.230**	.109	.212**
Workforce productivity	.357***	.049	.306***
Understanding of business issues	.279**	.169*	.141
Support for change	.279**	.079	.196*
Flexibility in work practices	.303***	.144	.273**
Speed of decision-making	.041	-. 121	.172*
Clarity re management's right to decide	-.076	-.206**	.034
Quality of strategic decisions	.196*	-.091	.375***
Effectiveness of implementation of strategic decisions	.145	.125	.280**
Quality of operational decisions	.220**	.022	.112
Effectiveness of implementation of operational decisions	.129	.073	.311***
Outcomes of Importance to Employees			
Management understanding of employee and trade union problems	.307***	-.023	.290**
Job satisfaction/employee morale	.190*	.058	.069
Security of employment	.156	.125	-.050
Staffing levels	-.060	-.085	-.081
Levels of pay and conditions	.107	.087	.077

Outcomes of Importance to Trade Unions			
Management involvement of the union	.138	.070	.127
Union influence on management decisions	.246**	.033	.247**
Outcomes for Workplace Relationships			
Quality of communications	.182*	.244**	.207**
Level of trust	.029	-.027	.164
Incidence of industrial disputes	-.111	-.065	-.202
Incidence of IR grievances	.015	-.046	-.215*

$* p < 0.1 ** p < 0.05 *** p < 0.01$

Partnership type appears to have a significant effect on only two of the five outcomes variables of importance to employees, i.e. management understanding of employee and trade union problems and job satisfaction. It does not appear to make any difference for security of employment, staffing levels, and levels of pay and conditions of employment. The table suggests that integrated exploratory partnerships have a somewhat stronger effect on these employee outcomes than integrated business partnerships and that both of these integrated partnership types have stronger effects than exploratory and business partnerships. There is no difference as far as these outcomes are concerned between business and exploratory or integrated exploratory partnerships.

Partnership type appears to have a significant effect on one of the two outcomes variables of importance to trade unions, i.e. union influence on management decision-making. Partnership type does not appear to make a difference for management involvement of the union on a day-to-day basis. The table suggests that both integrated exploratory and integrated business partnerships have broadly equal positive effects for union influence on management decision-making and that both of these integrated partnership types have stronger effects than exploratory and business partnerships. There is no difference as far as these outcomes are concerned between business and exploratory or integrated exploratory partnerships.

Partnership type appears to have a significant effect on two of the four outcomes variables for workplace relationships, which we consider to be of equal importance to management, employees and trade unions. These two variables are the quality of communications between managers/supervisors and representatives/employees and the incidence of industrial relations grievances. Partnership type does not appear to matter for levels of trust and incidence of industrial disputes. The table suggests that integrated business partnerships have a somewhat stronger effect on these relationships outcomes than integrated exploratory partnerships and that business partnerships have a somewhat stronger effect than exploratory and integrated exploratory partnerships.

Collective Bargaining Outcomes

Next we consider the effects of our partnership types on collective bargaining outcomes. Table 7.6 sets out the standardised beta coefficients for our partnership types and the dependent variables for the collective bargaining outcomes.

Partnership type appears to have a significant effect on four of the seven collective bargaining outcomes variables, i.e. whether the collective bargaining agenda is the same or has more or fewer items on it, whether issues that were previously handled through collective bargaining had been passed into the partnership system, whether the unions had put issues that in the past were handled by them through collective bargaining into the partnership process, and whether the effectiveness of collective bargaining has been improved by partnership.

Table 7.6: Regression Results: Partnership Types and Collective Bargaining Outcomes

Dependent Variables	Standardized Beta Coefficients		
	Integrated Exploratory Partnerships	*Business Partnerships*	*Integrated Business Partnerships*
Effects of partnership on collective bargaining			
Content of collective bargaining agenda	.267**	-.061	-.003
Issues passed from collective bargaining to partnership	.383***	.008	.235**
Issues covered by managerial prerogative passed to partnership	.148	.038	.103
Issues passed by unions from collective bargaining to partnership	.381***	.023	.231**
Is collective bargaining more or less adversarial	-.054	-.028	-.103
Effectiveness of collective bargaining	-.219**	.078	-.100
Ratification of partnership issues through collective bargaining	-.114	.083	-.021

* $p < 0.1$ ** $p < 0.05$ *** $p < 0.01$

Partnership type appears to make no difference for the remaining variables, i.e. whether issues covered in the past by managerial prerogative have been passed into partnership, whether collective bargaining is more or less adversarial and whether partnership issues have to be ratified through collective bargaining. The table suggests that integrated exploratory partnerships have a stronger positive effect on these outcomes than integrated business partnerships and that both integrated partnership types have stronger effects than exploratory and business partnerships. The latter appear to have no stronger effects than exploratory partnerships as far as these collective bargaining outcomes are concerned. It will be recalled that we did not include questions on future collective bargaining outcomes.

Conclusions on Current Outcomes

Taking all of the findings on current outcomes together it seems reasonable to come to a number of conclusions, again bearing in mind the small number of cases, especially with respect to business partnerships, and the consequent caution around statistical significance.

Firstly, it emerges, as we had expected, that exploratory partnerships appear to have the weakest overall influence on current outcomes generally. This appears to confirm the position of exploratory partnerships as the weakest of our four types in respect to outcomes.

Secondly, contrary to expectations, both integrated exploratory and integrated business partnerships have broadly equivalent positive effects for most current outcomes and stronger effects than either business or exploratory partnerships. That integrated exploratory partnerships had equivalent effects to integrated business partnerships and stronger effects than business partnerships runs counter to our expectations. It will be recalled that we had expected that our integrated business partnership type, which we had designated as our strongest type, would have the strongest positive effects of all four types.

Thirdly, and again contrary to our expectations, business partnerships appear to have a weaker effect across all categories of current outcomes than integrated exploratory and integrated business partnerships. This type appears broadly equivalent in terms of influence to our exploratory type.

Fourthly, on the issue of 'mutual gains', the findings on current outcomes suggest that both integrated exploratory and integrated business partnerships have stronger positive effects for outcomes of importance to management than for outcomes of importance to employees and trade unions. For example, both integrated types of partnership seem to have a positive effect on almost all the management outcomes including what might be considered key performance outcomes such as business performance, workforce productivity, union members' attitudes to change and union members' flexibility in work practices. On the other hand, they seem to have a positive effect on a fewer number of employee and trade union outcomes and to have no effect at all on job security, staffing levels and pay and conditions of employment all of which might be considered to be outcomes of major importance to employees and trade unions. Before discussing these conclusions in any further detail we need to report the finding on future outcomes, which we do in the section below.

Future Outcomes for Management, Employees and Trade Unions

It will be recalled that our findings relating to partnership in general showed that survey respondents had higher expectations of future outcomes than those achieved to date across all the outcomes measured. It will be recalled that we included questions about expected future outcomes because we were conscious of the very recent provenance of most of our cases.

Table 7.7 sets out the standardised beta coefficients for our partnership types and the dependent variables for future outcomes of importance to management, employees, and trade unions.

Partnership type appears to have a significant effect on all but five future outcomes variables. The exceptions are speed of decision making, clarity re management's right to make decisions, quality of operational decisions, security of employment and staffing levels. Partnership type appears to have a significant effect on eight of the eleven outcomes variables of importance to management, the only exceptions being speed of decision-making, clarity re management's right to decide and implementation of operational decisions.

Table 7.7: Regression Results: Partnership Types and Future Outcomes

Dependent Variables	Standardised Beta Coefficients		
	Integrated Exploratory Partnerships	*Business Partnerships*	*Integrated Business Partnerships*
Outcomes of Importance to Management			
Business performance	.070	.167*	.196*
Workforce productivity	.242**	.216**	204**
Union members' understanding of business issues	.074	.141	251**
Union members' support for change	.214**	.155*	409***
Union members' flexibility in work practices	.225**	.247**	.356***
Speed of decision making	.098	.000	.077
Clarity re management's right to decide	-.114	-.012	.087
Quality of strategic decisions	.189*	-.034	.246**
Implementation of strategic decisions	.067	-.024	.229**
Quality of operational decisions	.045	-.023	.020
Implementation of operational decisions	.045	-.013	.167*
Outcomes of Importance to Employees			
Management understanding of employee and trade union problems	.194*	.168*	.176*
Job satisfaction/employee morale	.018	-.012	.211**
Security of employment	-.134	.130	.057
Staffing levels	-.062	.000	-.079
Levels of pay and conditions of employment	.014	.201**	.273**

Outcomes of Importance to Trade Unions			
Management involvement of the union	.130	.200*	.268**
Union influence on management decisions	.253**	.144	.083
Outcomes for Workplace Relationships			
Quality of communications	.177*	.182*	.346***
Level of trust	.098	-.027	.243**
Incidence of industrial disputes	-.111	-.065	-.202*
Incidence of IR grievances from workforce	.015	-.046	-.215**

* $p <0.1$ ** $p <0.05$ *** $p <0.01$

Partnership type appears to have a significant effect on three of the five outcomes variables of importance to employees, the exceptions being security of employment and staffing levels. Partnership type appears to have a significant effect for future outcomes relating to levels of pay and conditions of employment but not, as we noted earlier, for current levels of pay and conditions. Integrated business partnerships appear to have more positive effects on these outcomes than each of the other three types.

Partnership type appears to have a significant effect on both of the outcomes variables of importance to trade unions, i.e. management involvement of the union on a day-to-day basis and union influence on management decisions. Both integrated partnership types appear to have more positive effects than the other two types.

Finally, partnership type appears to have a significant effect on all of the four outcomes variables for workplace relationships, which we considered to be of equal importance to management, employees and trade unions. Integrated business partnerships appear strongly to have more positive effects on these outcomes than each of the other three types.

The pattern of influence that emerges in this table is markedly different to the pattern that emerges in the regressions for current outcomes. In the case of expected future outcomes overall, integrated business partnerships show stronger effects than each of the other three types in the case of twelve of the twenty-three outcomes listed. Integrated exploratory partnerships show stronger effects than integrated business partnership in only one instance, union influence on management decisions. Integrated exploratory partnerships appear to have somewhat more positive effects than business partnerships and exploratory partnerships but significantly less positive effects than in the case of current outcomes.

In sum, bearing in mind the caveat relating to the small number of cases and the consequent caution around statistical significance, taking all of the findings on future outcomes together it seems reasonable to come to a number of broad conclusions.

Firstly, exploratory partnerships emerge again as the weakest form of partnership. Secondly, integrated exploratory partnerships appear to have weaker positive effects on future than on current outcomes. Thirdly, business partnerships emerge as having broadly equivalent effects to integrated exploratory partnerships and not weaker effects, as had been the case in respect to current outcomes. Fourthly, integrated business partnerships appear to have a stronger positive effect than each of the other three types across the range of outcomes of importance to management, employees and trade unions. Thus, it appears only in the case of future outcomes that there is strong support for our designation of this type of partnership as our strongest type in terms of outcomes.

Our final conclusion regarding the findings on future outcomes relates to the 'mutual gains' premise. While integrated business partnerships appear to have the strongest positive effects on outcomes for all parties there still seems to be a skew towards management in terms of benefits. We saw that integrated business partnerships had the strongest positive effects on several outcomes of importance to management but that it did not seem to make a difference as far as security of employment and staffing levels were concerned. Thus we can see that the pattern of influence of the four partnership types is considerably different – except as far as exploratory partnerships are concerned – in terms of future as opposed to current outcomes. In the next section we seek to explain these findings by drawing on the international and Irish literatures.

Discussion of Partnership Types and Current and Future Outcomes

Current Outcomes

The findings relating to current outcomes imply that the structure dimension of partnership, as we have defined it (i.e. whether cases have strategic or operational bodies only or whether they have both), has more influence than content as we have defined it (i.e. whether cases have a light or a weighty mainstream agenda). Both integrated partnership types have strategic and operational bodies but our integrated exploratory partnerships had less than half the average number of agenda items that our integrated business type had, 15 agenda items compared to 31.

Both types emerged as having broadly equivalent positive effects on current outcomes and there does not appear to be any 'dividend' for the additional agenda items that integrated business partnerships had.

One line of explanation for why structures might matter more than content as an influence on current outcomes might be found in the attention given by researchers to the importance of having multiple partnership structures with linkages between them for the development of the type of sound workplace relationships that are needed to support partnership (Cutcher-Gershenfeld and Verma, 1994; Kochan and Osterman, 1994; Guest and Peccei, 2001). We know that developing partnership is far from easy, especially where relationships are of a low trust, adversarial kind and that considerable internal and external helps are frequently needed to sustain developments (Cooke, 1990). Hence management and unions place considerable emphasis in the early phases of partnership on getting agreed structures, ground rules and ways of working in place (Herrick, 1985).

The argument here is that engagement between managers, employees and union representatives at different levels of organisation can help to develop the co-operative relationships, trust and problem solving skills needed to address important organisational problems that affect all parties. As seen earlier, Cooke (1990) distinguishes between improvements in company performance that are brought about directly through improved productivity, product quality, and efficiency or indirectly through improved relationships between managers, supervisors, employees and union representatives.

As we have seen, bringing management and unions together in partnership can lead to improved relationships, increased trust, a better atmosphere at work, information sharing, more dialogue, less adversarialism, more positive attitudes towards change, and the identification of areas of joint concern (Heckscher, 1988: 150; HRDC, 1998; Marks et al., 1998; Marchington, 1992; Clarke and Haiven, 1999). Such 'relationships' outcomes may be seen as 'direct' outcomes of effective joint working. These outcomes may also have an 'indirect' effect in that, for example, improved communications and higher levels of trust can create a sound relationship which parties can then use to identify and address problems associated with productivity and quality that have definite 'bottom line' implications (Cooke, 1990: 589). Indeed, it may be argued that improved relationships and attitudinal change must occur through relationships building and joint working in committees and other groups before significant issues can be addressed through partnership (Schuster, 1984; Verma and Cutcher-Gershenfeld, 1993).

For these reasons, then, it may be that the current outcomes of our integrated exploratory and integrated business partnerships were more the product of structures and the engagement that takes place through them than the product of the agendas concerned. It may be that structures facilitate outcomes both directly through the agendas being addressed and indirectly through 'climate setting' that facilitates higher levels of co-operation from employees and trade unions and the opening up of more contentious and difficult agendas over time.

It could also be the case that structure is picking up something of the impact of content on outcomes and that the two dimensions we used to define our four partnership types were not as distinct from one another as we had supposed. It will be recalled that we defined strategic and operational bodies both by the levels of organisation at which we expected them to operate and by the types of agendas that we considered would typify such bodies. Or it may be that content is actually more important than the findings appear to suggest but that our distinction between agendas on the basis of their numbers of mainstream items may be too rudimentary to capture more subtle distinctions among them. For example, it may be that some agenda items have greater potential for delivering results than others and that having a small number of such agenda items may be more significant than a large number of items with less potential.

It could be the case that formulating agenda items with simple phrases such as 'introduction of new organisation structures' or 'plans to introduce new forms of work organisation' masks significant differences between what organisations might be considering under such 'generic' headings. Also, we did not distinguish between items that were still on the agenda as opposed to items that had been removed through disagreement or agreement to act on them. It was not possible to take such finer distinctions into account in a survey of this type and so we may have failed to capture the full importance of agenda as an influence on current outcomes.

Another line of explanation for why structures might matter more than content as an influence on current outcomes might be that other factors that we have not measured have important influences on partnership outcomes. We have already seen that Cooke (1990), for example, concludes that the factors likely to influence outcomes such as company performance and management-union relations are related to what he terms 'intensity of joint efforts' or the amount of time, effort, commitment and the quality of input to joint activities. We do not consider that it would have been possible in a survey of this type to gather reliable data on factors such as the levels of commitment of parties or the level of quality of their inputs to meetings and other activities. But the results are consistent with the possibility that integrated structures induce a 'high intensity' of effort and that this could be a significant influence on outcomes.

Current Outcomes and the Mutual Gains Premise

The next issue for consideration is the 'mutual gains' issue as this emerges in the findings for current outcomes. The findings suggested that both integrated exploratory and integrated business partnerships have stronger positive effects for outcomes of importance to management than for outcomes of importance to employees and trade unions. Both integrated types of partnership seemed to have a positive effect on almost all management outcomes but not on all employee and trade union outcomes.

In general the findings on outcomes for employees and trade unions and for workplace relationships appear consistent with research findings internationally around benefits such as more information from management and better communications, higher investment in training and development, increased job satisfaction, and some degree of influence over workplace issues (Kochan et al., 1984; Marchington, 1992; Batt and Applebaum,

1995; Marks et al., 1998; HRDC, 1998; Clarke and Haiven, 1999). The finding that partnership type does make a difference for union influence on management decisions is positive for trade unions and employees and this outcome appears more important than the other trade union outcomes of management involvement of the union on a day-to-day basis.

It is possible, however, that these findings underestimate the benefits of partnership to employees and trade unions by the way in which we have categorised most outcomes as being primarily of importance either to management or to employees and trade unions. For example, there is evidence that the issues of most concern to union members are not confined to those we had cited but extend to working in co-operation with management and the future of the company (Geary, 2006). It is also worth noting evidence that when partnership yields positive outcomes for employees, that unions appear to receive an indirect benefit in the form of greater membership commitment which is an outcome that we could not realistically measure in a survey being answered by senior managers (Geary, 2006; Roche and Geary, 2006).

Nevertheless, it seems reasonable to conclude that even our strong partnership types are likely to make more of a difference on current outcomes of importance to management than on outcomes of importance to employees and trade unions. This finding runs counter to our expectations and to the optimism of the 'mutual gains' literature (Kochan and Osterman, 1994; Applebaum et al., 2000). The finding is, however, consistent with other findings that have described the limitations on employee and trade union gains alongside significant gains for management as 'constrained mutuality' (Guest and Peccei, 2001; Osterman, 2001; Kelly, 2004).

Future Outcomes

In the case of expected future outcomes, integrated business partnerships emerged as the strongest type with effects across the range of outcomes of importance to management, employees and trade unions that were stronger than the other three types. This implies, then, that the weighty agendas of our integrated business partnerships achieve a dividend over integrated exploratory partnerships with their light agenda that they did not achieve in the case of current outcomes. We need to consider, therefore, why this might be the case.

The likelihood is that we can explain why the weighty agendas of our integrated business partnerships achieved a dividend over integrated exploratory partnerships in respect to future outcomes by looking to the factors that we used to discuss why structure appeared to matter more than content in terms of influence on current outcomes. In that discussion we saw that a number of factors had been identified in the international literature as being important to the success of partnership. These included the importance of having multiple partnership structures and the development of sound workplace relationships.

In the case of integrated business partnerships that had twice the number of agenda items as integrated exploratory partnerships it might be expected that it would take longer to develop the structures and relationships needed to ensure that the parties could develop and handle such weighty agendas. We saw that there was evidence that partnership programmes took time to mature and realise their full capacity for improved performance (Schuster, 1983; Cooke, 1990).

In such circumstances, respondents with weighty agendas in particular would be unlikely to be in a position early in the life of the partnership to point to significant outcomes as having been already achieved. Knowing, however, that they had a weighty agenda of mainstream issues and having confidence in their structures and processes, it seems reasonable that they would expect future outcomes to be of a magnitude not achieved to date. In this situation it appears reasonable that agenda would matter more in the case of future outcomes than in the case of current outcomes.

We have already seen that at the time the survey was conducted almost eight out of ten cases were about three to four years old and about half were only two to three years old. Our survey asked if items had been on the agenda within the past six months and did not ask if these items had been resolved or otherwise moved to an action stage. It may be the case, then, that while items were on agendas, sufficient time had not elapse for these items to be resolved let alone implemented.

Future Outcomes and the Mutual Gains Premise

Finally, it also appears that there is a balance in favour of management as opposed to employees in the division of future benefits from partnership but to a somewhat lesser extent than in the case of current outcomes. This finding is striking in that it suggests that even in regard to future outcomes, those involved expected partnership to fall somewhat short of delivering fully on 'mutual gains' (Kochan and Osterman, 1994; Guest and Peccei, 2001). Integrated business partnerships were associated with positive outcomes relating to future but not current levels of pay and conditions and relating to future but not current management involvement of the union on a day-to-day basis. Even integrated business partnerships were not, however, associated with more positive effects on future job security and staffing levels any more than for current outcomes around these key employee and trade union concerns.

When it comes to future outcomes of mutual importance to management and employees and trade unions the picture seems somewhat more positive. Again, integrated business partnerships appeared to have a significant effect on all of the four outcomes variables affecting workplace relationships (quality of communications, level of trust, incidence of industrial disputes, and incidence of industrial relations grievances from the workforce).

Nevertheless, it seems reasonable to conclude that in the case of expected future outcomes there still appears to be a balance of advantage in the direction of management but to a somewhat lesser degree. We have already concluded that competitive reality limits the capacity of partnership to deliver on job security for employees over the longer run. In sum, even in respect to expected future outcomes, our integrated business partnership appears to be limited to delivering a 'constrained mutuality', albeit a less 'constrained mutuality' than was found to be the case in respect to current outcomes.

The findings in respect to future outcomes imply that it is possible to structure partnerships, for example by ensuring that they have both strategic and operational bodies as well as weighty agendas, such that more equal benefits can be expected to accrue to management, employees and trade unions. This implies that it would be in the interest of both management and trade unions to encourage the development of integrated business partnerships, as we have defined them here.

Summary and Conclusions

In this chapter we classified our partnership cases into four types which we called 'exploratory', 'integrated exploratory', 'business' and 'integrated business'. In exploring whether or not different sets of circumstances might lead to the emergence of different types of partnership, we combined our 'exploratory' and 'integrated exploratory' types into a single 'exploratory' type and we combined our 'business' and 'integrated business' types into a single 'business' type. We found that two different sets of circumstances were associated in the main with these two types but not in the precise manner that we had expected. We also sought to explore whether or not some types of partnership lead to better outcomes and, indeed, 'mutual gains' for employers, employees and trade unions. We extended this part of the exploration to all four types. We found that in the case of current outcomes, both 'integrated exploratory' and 'integrated business' types outperformed the others. This suggested that as far as current outcomes were concerned, structure mattered more than content and we discussed why this might be the case. We found that in the case of current outcomes partnership type mattered more for outcomes of importance to management than to outcomes of importance to employees and trade unions. We found in the case of future outcomes that our 'integrated business' type outperformed the other three, thus implying that in respect to future outcomes, content mattered more than structure. We also found in respect to future outcomes that partnership type mattered more for outcomes of importance to management than for outcomes of importance to employees and trade unions. We concluded that in respect to both current and future outcomes, partnership had delivered a constrained degree of 'mutual gains'.

8

CONCLUSIONS AND FUTURE PROSPECTS

In this chapter we provide a short summary of the main findings from our research including an update on the demise and survival of the cases some ten years later. We discuss some of the implications of our research for policy makers and for practitioners. We consider the prospects for the wider development of workplace partnership in the private sector in the context of the current economic recession which now places considerable additional pressures on employers and trade unions. Finally, we provide some thoughts on the legacy of this 'first generation' of workplace partnerships in Ireland.

Main Findings

Partnership and Organisational Change

It will be recalled that we defined partnership as an approach to organisational change in the unionised sector that involved management, employees and union representatives working co-operatively on issues of mutual concern using structures and processes separate from existing collective bargaining arrangements.

The Organisations

The main findings on the organisations that took part in the survey including the reasons given for adopting partnership were:

- Most cases developed between 1997 and 2000 in very specific public policy circumstances; particularly influential were national programmes especially *Partnership 2000* and EU-funded projects that IBEC, ICTU, IPC and SIPTU sponsored;

- More than half of all cases were private sector manufacturing firms, more than a quarter were in the services sector, and only about 10 per cent of cases were from the public services;

- Most cases involved large and long-established organisations;

- The most common reason cited for adopting partnership was the anticipation of significant future changes. Second in importance was the need for further investment;

- In most cases trade union density was between 51 and 100 per cent, higher than the national average, with high degrees of union involvement in day-to-day operations;

- In most cases the overall quality of management-union-employee relationships was low to moderate and the level of trust was low;

- There was considerable satisfaction with collective bargaining as far as pay and conditions went but dissatisfaction as far as the handling of change was concerned;

- Finally, the findings showed a moderate to high degree of support for partnership among managers and full-time union officials albeit with lower levels of support among middle than top management;

Partnership Structures and Agendas

The main findings on partnership structures and agendas were:

- Partnership structures broadly followed the 'two-tiered' US pattern. More than half of all cases had strategic partnership bodies and more than eight out of ten had operational bodies;

- Agendas focussed more on 'hard' issues such as financial performance, changes in work practices etc than on 'soft' issues such as communications and relationships;

- Most agendas reflected the concerns of management and unions. However, agendas tended to focus to a greater extent on issues of concern to management than to employees and trade unions;

- Issues of importance to employees and trade unions such as job security and staffing levels featured very low down in order of importance on partnership agendas;

- Industrial relations issues were not precluded from partnership agendas in most cases.

Outcomes for Employers, Employees and Trade Unions

The main findings on the current outcomes of partnership for employers, employees and trade unions were:

- In most cases business performance, workforce productivity, union members' understanding of business issues, union members' flexibility and support for change were higher;

- There was no evidence that partnership either slowed decision-making down or caused confusion around managerial authority;

- In most cases management understanding of employee and trade union problems was higher;

- Less than half the respondents considered that security of employment was higher as a result of partnership. Slightly more than half considered that job satisfaction and pay and conditions were higher;

- Partnership had no obvious effect on staffing levels;

- In most cases there were positive outcomes in terms of union influence on management decision-making and management involvement of the union;

- There appeared to be no negative outcomes for trade unions;

- In most cases there were positive relationships outcomes, e.g. the quality of communications and level of trust;

- In most cases the incidence of industrial disputes and grievances was lower, and collective bargaining was more effective and less adversarial;

- Taken together, the findings confirmed that through partnership management, employees and trade unions could achieve positive outcomes, i.e. 'mutual gains';

- However, benefits appeared to be skewed somewhat in favour of management as opposed to employees.

- In addition, the full potential of the partnerships had not yet been realised and most respondents expected more from partnership in future than had been achieved to date.

Findings on Partnership Types

The main findings on whether or not different sets of circumstances influenced the emergence of different types of partnership and whether or not different types of partnership led to different outcomes were:

- As we had expected, most 'business' partnerships developed in 'turbulent' circumstances characterised by a combination of strong external and internal influences. However, contrary to our expectations, more than half of our 'exploratory' partnerships also developed in similar circumstances. We then needed to explain why 'weak' 'exploratory' partnerships might develop in the same circumstances as 'strong' 'business' partnerships. The most cogent explanations lay in the influence of factors that we had not included in the survey such as senior management and trade union leadership, third party facilitation, and training and development supports.

- In terms of partnership types and outcomes, we found that, contrary to our expectations, partnership structures mattered more than partnership agendas in influencing current outcomes. This became evident when we found that 'integrated exploratory' and 'integrated business' types led to better outcomes than 'exploratory' and 'business' types. We needed to explain this unexpected finding. We looked at how structures facilitated engagement at different levels of organisation and how structures could accelerate the development of the trust and problem solving skills needed if management, employees and trade unions were to address significant change agendas together.

- In the case of future expected outcomes, we found that our 'strongest' type, i.e. 'integrated business' partnerships had the most significant outcomes of the four types.

- The findings on current outcomes suggested that both 'integrated exploratory' and 'integrated business' partnerships had stronger positive effects for outcomes of importance to management than for outcomes of importance to employees and trade unions. In the case of expected future outcomes, we found that 'integrated business' partnerships also had stronger positive effects for outcomes of importance to management than for outcomes of importance to employees or trade unions. We concluded that there was a limited or 'constrained' degree of mutuality in terms of outcomes.

How Does Partnership Help Organisational Change?

These findings establish that partnership can provide a distinctive approach to organisational change in the unionised sector that can bring significant benefits to employers, employees and trade union. From the survey findings and from the short case studies, it emerges that partnership can help the parties to handle organisational changes effectively in a number of ways.

Through the initial discussions on partnership, sometimes involving formal diagnosis of organisational problems and workplace relationships, management and unions identify the importance for all parties of having effective change management arrangements in place. The partnership structures allow management to raise organisational change issues in a non-adversarial environment without risking immediate trade union opposition, as commonly happens when such issues are raised through the adversarial industrial relations procedures. For their part, union representatives and employees have the facility to explore and to question the rationale for and implications of proposed changes in a detailed and non-adversarial manner. They also have an opportunity to influence decisions on proposed changes. In addition, they generally have the 'safety net' of being able to take controversial issues on which it is not possible to make progress into the industrial relations procedures for further discussion and negotiation.

Through partnership the parties can improve mutual understanding, including understanding of business issues and employees' concerns, and can improve workplace relationships including trust levels. Partnership gives the unions the facility to bring a 'mutual gains' dimension into the change process. They can raise employee concerns and demands in a manner that allows them to be considered by management without the unions necessarily having to formulate them as industrial relations claims. Where unions assert their members' concerns and demands in the form of industrial relations claims they are frequently resisted by management and can become the source of local divisiveness.

Management and trade unions can decide which issues they are willing to address through partnership and which issues they are willing to address through industrial relations bargaining. By working both channels effectively the parties can reduce the areas of contention and make their bargaining more effective and less adversarial. Partnership and industrial relations can have positive 'spill over' effects on each other.

Partnership can facilitate achievement of the 'ownership' of organisational change that textbooks on change insist is essential for success. It also facilitates wider knowledge and ideas inputs on the part of those most likely to be affected by changes and who will be responsible for implementing changes. Having formal partnership arrangements also facilitates the development of new knowledge and skills in areas such as organisational change, business understanding, meetings, conflict resolution, negotiation and joint problem solving.

In light of the finding that partnership 'works' as a distinctive approach to organisational change and has positive outcomes for employers, employees and trade unions, a number of questions arise. Why have few employers and trade unions in the private sector adopted workplace partnership since the early 2000s? What are the prospects for the wider diffusion of partnership over the coming years in the private sector? What enduring legacy, if any, has been left by this 'first generation' of workplace partnerships? Before addressing these questions we need to report on the de-mise and survival of our cases.

The Demise and Survival of the Partnership Cases

Nine years on what do we know of the survival of our cases? Over 2008/2009 we sought to establish through telephone contacts whether partnership structures were still in place and, if not, what the reasons were for their demise. It will be recalled that a small number of cases (8) had already ended before the survey. Four respondents cited industrial relations difficulties, one cited a management decision, two cited a trade union decision and one gave no reason. In Table 8.1 we summarise the main findings from this follow up survey of the 88 cases that we used in the research.

Table 8.1 Status of Cases in 2008/2009

Still Operational	Ended Before Survey	Ended Due to Closure	Ended Due to IR Reasons	Don't Know
35	5	16	13	19
39.8%	5.7%	18.2%	14.8%	21.6%

Almost four out of ten cases (39.8 per cent) were still operational, about two in ten (18.2 per cent) had ended because of the closure of the companies concerned, less than two in ten (14.8 per cent) had ended due to industrial relations difficulties, and it was not possible to establish the current status with certainty of a little more than two cases out of ten (21.6 per cent). That as few as 15 per cent of cases ended due to industrial relations reasons might be seen as significant given what we know of the low trust, adversarial contexts in which most partnerships were grounded.

We saw in Chapter 3 that the survival rates of employee involvement initiatives appear to be low with estimates of attrition rates varying from about one in ten (Cooke, 1990: 63) to up to two thirds after six years (Kochan and Osterman, 1994). It is clearly a major challenge for employers and trade unions not just to establish partnerships but also to sustain them over time and to embed them as day-to-day practice (Kochan and Dyer, 1976: 69; Kochan et al., 1984: 11).

We don't have detailed information as to why about 15 per cent of the cases ended due to industrial relations reasons. In one case the management respondent said that the degree of adversarialism had declined significantly over the years as the company shrank from 600 to 100 employees. He said that competitive pressures had left no time for partnership and that instead of involving the union in organisational change the company had opted for direct employee involvement in lean manufacturing. Another respondent explained the demise of partnership by a low degree of trade union 'buy in' to organisational change with major projects not being completed. He said that these projects were later 're-formatted' and implemented 'through management control'. In another case the manager stated that shop stewards withdrew from partnership because industrial relations issues could not be discussed. Later, when the company faced possible closure, a joint discussion forum was reinstated that subsequently endured after the survival issues had been resolved.

In the case of Aer Rianta, Roche and Geary (2006) concluded that the absence of a process for bringing issues in dispute within partnership into 'mutual gains bargaining' led to situations where the parties, absent a viable alternative means of resolving disputes, simply retreated back into adversarial collective bargaining. Sometimes partnerships are suspended for a period of time, for example when a trade union decides to withdraw. Such withdrawals are invariably related to industrial relations developments. In eircom, for example, it was reported that the Communications Workers Union (CWU) withdrew temporarily from the partnership system due to what it perceived as delays in securing recognition in a subsidiary company, Meteor (IRN, 30 August 2006).

We also saw a number of explanations for why partnerships might end in the literature on partnership. The external and internal conditions that stimulated the decision to adopt partnership may change to such an extent as to significantly weaken the pressure on the parties to remain engaged. For example, a crisis might be overcome and the pressures to co-operate may then abate. Or changed conditions may make it difficult for the parties to continue to attain valued goals, for example the joint sharing of gains if economic conditions worsen (Kochan and Dyer, 1976). Management and unions may be willing to co-operate when economic conditions are bad but then lose interest when circumstances improve (HRDC, 1998).

Changes in the relative strengths of the parties may also be a factor. It can be extremely difficult for employers and trade unions to resist the use of power when they become convinced that they can achieve more through power than through partnership (Hammer and Stern, 1986: 337-338; Cooke, 1990: 40). Rankin and Mansell (1986) argue that the very nature of 'parallel' partnership structures makes them easy to dismantle. The voluntary character of partnership may also lead to inherent instability (Streeck, 1992).

Partnerships may also fall foul of organisational politics (Kochan et al., 1984: 11). Middle managers and highly skilled employees such as craft workers are likely to resist any diminution of their power (Fenton-O'Creevy, 1998: 68; McKersie, 2002: 113; Kochan et al., 1984: 47; Clarke and Haiven, 1999: 175; Harrison et al., 2001; Roche and Geary, 2006). In Aer Rianta, middle management involvement in the development of partnership was very limited and they generally viewed partnership as a threat to their role (Roche and Geary, 2006).

In their study of partnership in Waterford Glass and Aughinish Alumina, Gunnigle and Dobbins (2009: 568) highlighted a number of factors as likely to underpin the durability of partnerships, including relative insulation from market forces, continuity in top management and union support, internal institutionalisation of partnership arrangements, and capital intensive process technology. The Aer Rianta case also supports the view that continuity in top management and trade union leadership and support is important to success (Roche and Geary, 2006).

In Exhibits 1 and 2 we outline two partnerships that came to an end, one temporarily, Bausch and Lomb, and the other permanently, Aer Rianta.

A US company, Bausch and Lomb began operations in Waterford in 1981 with 200 employees. For a period of time the company appears to have been insulated to a degree from market forces. In the early 1980s the company had no serious competitors but by the end of the decade several new companies had entered the market (Teague and Hann, 2008). In 2009 the lens plant had 1,400 employees the majority of whom were members of SIPTU (operator grades) and TEEU (craft workers). In 2007 Warburg Pincus, a global private equity firm acquired Bausch and Lomb. The company has two plants, one manufacturing sunglasses and the other contact lenses.

The Bausch and Lomb lens plant partnership was one of the earliest to come to public attention (IRN, 29 January 1998, 26 March 1998, 30 April 1998, 6 October 1999, 9 September 2004, 18 August 2005, 27 January 2009). The context was one of an increasing need on the part of management for organisational changes and awareness that negotiating changes in the traditional manner meant that potential gains were frequently eroded by the time required to implement them.

The Bausch and Lomb case highlights the difficulty of changing an embedded adversarial industrial relations culture even during times when employment and pay levels were growing and where management and unions were working together through a formal partnership structure. Ultimately, it seems that neither management nor trade unions were willing to discard established adversarial approaches in the manner needed to sustain partnership (Teague and Hann, 2008). At the same time, the case highlights the ability of management and unions, with assistance from the LRC and Labour Court, to overcome their industrial relations difficulties and to recast 'partnership' in a different guise, i.e. as an information and consultation mechanism. The initial partnership developed as a voluntary management-union arrangement in keeping with *Partnership 2000*. Partnership now appears to be developing into a statutory information and consultation forum in keeping with the Employees (Provision of Information and Consultation) Act 2006.

Aer Rianta, until its dissolution into three separate entities in 2003, was Ireland's single state-owned airports authority. The company had a tradition of positive industrial relations and progressive HR policies. It employed some 3,300 staff between Dublin, Shannon and Cork with an overall union density level of over 90 per cent. The partnership arrangements in Aer Rianta – see Exhibit 2 – have been described as among the most far-reaching of their kind in promoting union and employee involvement in operational and strategic decision making at multiple levels (IRN, 24 July 2003; IRN, 19 November 2003; Roche and Geary, 2006). 'Constructive Participation' or 'CP' was the term used to describe partnership in Aer Rianta. The Department of Public Enterprise funded CP.

The case highlights the extent to which management and unions can develop multi-level, direct and indirect, participation arrangements through which they can address a wide range of operational and strategic issues. The case also highlights the degree of success that can be achieved through such arrangements. However, the case shows how even carefully designed and well-resourced partnerships can be undermined by internal dynamics, structural weaknesses and changes in ownership and legal status.

Exhibit 8.1: Bausch and Lomb

In 1995 there were serious difficulties in the lens plant in Waterford. Workers rejected a plan for change and management questioned the future of the company. In 1998 there was a major investment programme and a new partnership agreement in line with Partnership 2000. Between these dates, the management and unions worked together with the help of an IPC facilitator. The partnership agreement noted that participation was separate from collective bargaining. However, the parties hoped the new arrangements could help to avoid industrial relations difficulties. A staff survey showed positive attitudes towards the company but found that the unions should be given more involvement in the change process. The same year there was a dispute over organisational changes. The union claimed pay for change and the company insisted it had to go ahead with the changes even without agreement. This dispute was averted through the Labour Court. In 1999 plant management negotiated an agreement with SIPTU which included gainsharing and an industrial peace/binding arbitration clause. In 2004 SIPTU members voted to withdraw from the partnership arrangements. SIPTU said there was insufficient consultation, that issues of concern to workers were not being adequately addressed, and that partnership was on the employers' terms only. In 2006 an LRC report found that most workers were satisfied with pay and conditions but not with the way that changes were being handled. The report said that workers recognised the importance of co-operating with change but expressed dissatisfaction with the way in which management and unions dealt with change. In 2008, with the partnership agreement still 'on ice', management and unions negotiated a new 'information and consultation forum'. In 2009 management and SIPTU agreed a new two-year industrial peace agreement. The company also committed itself to the earliest meaningful involvement of employees and unions in the change process.

Exhibit 8.2: Aer Rianta

In 1988 three worker directors were elected to the AR Board. In 1991, a 'Joint Union Company Group' (JUCG) on participation was established. During 1994-95, the JUCG agreed a 'Compact for Constructive Participation' (CP). The agreement stated that no party would seek to impose unilateral change and that proposals for change would go through an agreed process involving those affected prior to any decisions. The JUCG acted as a 'steering group' for the CP process. CP envisaged a clear-cut division between partnership and collective bargaining. Parties could decide to handle an issue through CP and still retain the right to subsequently take the issue through collective bargaining. Or they could agree issues through CP and not use collective bargaining. Or they could simply use collective bargaining from the outset. A senior trade union official was seconded to CP and he and a key senior manager became the main champions. Full-time facilitators and extensive training were provided. Strategy Groups (SGs) and Significant Issue Groups (SIGs) were established to address issues such as maintenance and cleaning services, and the future of duty-free shops. Through engagement in the SGs management and unions effectively subsumed collective bargaining. They reached consensus on some key issues including a strategy for the future of AR. Worker Directors opposed this strategy. While most senior managers supported CP, not all did. Middle managers were brought into opposition by their trade union. CP did not effectively facilitate channelling of unresolved issues into a compatible form of negotiation such as 'mutual gains bargaining' or into other mechanisms for reaching finality. As a result, the parties fell back on collective bargaining and the state industrial relations agencies, although there had been some in-house mediation/arbitration. CP resources were devoted to strategic/representative initiatives to the detriment of operational/direct initiatives that might have benefited employees on the ground more. When champions of CP left the company the process was left exposed.

Implications of Findings for Practitioners and Policymakers

Because our findings showed that partnership led to overall positive outcomes for all parties, they provide justification for further initiatives on the part of employers and trade unions at workplace level. Our research suggests that where employers and trade unions decide to develop a partnership approach to organisational change they should take account of some key findings.

Our findings suggest strongly that partnership structures and agendas make a significant difference in terms of outcomes. If this is true, then it follows that management and trade unions can design partnership systems such that they have greater rather than less potential to deliver significant gains. In particular, it is open to them to design partnerships along the lines of our 'strongest' type, i.e. 'integrated business' partnership. Another relevant finding was that 'mutual gains' may be skewed towards management to the comparative disadvantage of employees. This suggests that in agenda setting the parties need to ensure that the interests of employees are made explicit and that agendas are developed that are capable of delivering better pay and conditions and a better quality of working life as well as organisational performance improvements.

Also of relevance is our finding that there was a greater likelihood of partnership delivering significant benefits over the long rather than the short term. This finding has practical implications too. For example, in goal setting management and unions at local level are commonly inclined to go for 'quick wins' but the findings suggest that aspiring to bigger wins over a longer timeframe will also be needed.

The findings also provide justification for further initiatives on the wider diffusion of partnership in the workplace from the social partners and state agencies such as the NCPP and LRC. One of the key assumptions underpinning public policy on partnership to date has been the view that no one type or model of partnership could produce more significant outcomes than others (NESC, 1996; Government of Ireland, 1997; O'Donnell and Teague, 2000). This assumption no longer holds water in light of our findings on the importance of agendas and structures in delivering significant outcomes. We have also seen the difficulties in sustaining partnership over time. An issue, therefore, for public policy must be the design of supports that can be delivered over a period of say three to five years or more rather than over a shorter period of time. We also saw that industrial relations difficulties could undermine partnership arrangements. This too is a factor that needs to be taken into account in the design of support services from NCPP and LRC.

Workplace Partnership in 2009

Irish governments have accepted that co-operative work relations are vital for economic progress and for the so-called 'knowledge economy'. In addition, the promotion of partnership by governments and the social partners, assumed that the traditional adversarial approach to workplace change was not 'fit for purpose' in an increasingly competitive and globalised economy. We saw that since the 1990s, trade unions acknowledged the limitations of the adversarial model for both employers and trade unions (ICTU, 1993 and 1995). Consequently, partnership was advocated as an effective means of handling organisational change alongside established industrial relations machinery in the unionised sector. Notwithstanding the impressive efforts made by government, state industrial relations institutions and the social partners over the period 1997-2009 to promote partnership as an approach to organisational change, there is no evidence of widespread adoption of partnership in the private sector after 2000.

It is worth noting that many, if not most, of the cases that have been used to promote partnership and information and consultation arrangements in recent years are of a 1997-2000 vintage. Examples include Aughinish Alumina, Aer Rianta, Tegral Metal, AIB and Allianz. New cases that have been highlighted in more recent years include Beckman Coulter, a unionised company in Galway; Dell Ireland, a non-union company in Kildare; Medtronic, a unionised company in Galway; the Electric Paper Company, a non-union company in Dublin; GE Interlogix, a unionised company in Dublin; Multis, a non-union company in Galway; Roches Stores, a unionised company with stores nationwide at the time (since sold) (NCPP, 2004c); and Tesco Ireland, a unionised company with stores nationwide (IRN, 23 June 2005).

In addition, some 'headline' cases such as Waterford Glass (Dobbins, 2008) and Aer Rianta have collapsed (Roche, 2006). This has led one experienced commentator so suggest that instead of representing the beginning of a new era in Irish industrial relations, the 1997-2000 partnerships may, in fact, have been the 'high tide' of such developments (Roche, 2006). In the words of another commentator, the promise of widespread development of partnerships at workplace level building strong micro-foundations to the national system of social partnership appears not to have been realised (Teague and Hann, 2008). On the evidence, it seems reasonable now to abandon the idea that Ireland might develop a new national model of employment relations based on partnership between management, employees and unions (McKersie, 2002).

How might we explain the weak diffusion of workplace partnership in the private sector in light of the degree of social partner support and in light of the evidence that partnership can deliver significant gains to employers, employees and trade unions? A number of explanations can be offered.

As we have seen, it takes a particular confluence of external and internal circumstances to convince management and trade unions to take on the risks of departing from traditional 'low trust' assumptions about each other and to take on co-operative behaviours. Gunnigle and Dobbins (2009: 568) concluded that it requires quite special conditions for management to insulate workplace productivity coalitions from market turbulence and to balance conflict and co-operation. Teague and Hann (2008: 27) have concluded that in many cases neither management nor union representatives seem prepared to leave behind established employee relations behaviours and that, in any event, it is very difficult to get a stable, institutional form of co-operation that balances effectively the two approaches for a sustained period of time.

A study of organisational change and employee information and consultation systems found that the main obstacles to the development of information and consultation were short-term business pressures, a lack of time among line managers, and in some cases a bureaucratic culture that was resistant to change (Dundon et al. 2003).

The fact that many of our cases emerged in the context of a national programme that included a local bargaining clause in the private sector and in the context of EU-funded schemes suggests that national frameworks and funding and other supports are important. It seems reasonable to conclude that for employees and trade unions, access to productivity related additional payments was an important incentive to adoption of partnership and that for management, access to funding for consulting, training and facilitation supports was an important incentive to adopt partnership. However, it appears unlikely that employers will want further local bargaining clauses in national programmes and the funding that had been available through the EU's ADAPT programme has now been terminated. Indeed recent developments cast doubt on whether or not the current model of social partnership and national pay agreements will continue beyond the current year (IRN, 29 July 2009).

We have also seen that there has been a fragmentation of the national model of industrial relations into a number of alternative models since the 1980s (Roche, 1996), including an increase in the number of companies opting to be 'union-free' (Mooney, 2005). Employers who are seeking to make productivity gains and to elicit high commitment from their employees have available to them a range of possible approaches, even within the unionised sector. Put simply, many employers may not see the need for partnership given the availability of less costly and time-consuming alternatives (Gunnigle and Dobbins, 2009). Rapidly rising inward migration has also provided employers with a ready supply of relatively low-cost and sometimes compliant labour (Roche, 2006b).

There has been anecdotal evidence for some years now that there is a significant distancing on the part of many managers and union representatives from the term 'partnership'. The reason for this seems to be that both managers and trade unionists consider the term to be an over-statement of the degree of shared goal-setting and shared decision-making that generally takes place in workplace partnerships. Many managers and trade unionists appear to be more comfortable with what they often term 'joint working' or 'informal' collaborative arrangements. There are instances where employers and trade unions have opted not to use any terms to describe joint initiatives around specific issues on the grounds that this helps to avoid unnecessary controversy over 'partnership'.

In the case of Bausch and Lomb, the parties sought to ensure that a new co-operative agreement to replace the earlier partnership agreement did not have the term 'partnership' attached to it as 'both management and unions were of the view that the term partnership had become so sullied that it would be counterproductive to use it' (Teague and Hann, 2008: 21). It is worth noting that the LRC uses the term 'joint working' and not 'partnership' to describe structured forms of co-operation between management and trade unions. The LRC facilitates joint initiatives aimed at improving relationships, the conduct of industrial relations generally and the resolution of specific workplace issues.

It seems reasonable to conclude that the very limited spread of partnership in the private sector has not been a consequence of inadequate effort or resources on the part of those promoting partnership. Instead it seems reasonable to conclude that the limited development of partnership is more credibly explained by reference to more powerful forces such as the underlying strength and resilience of the adversarial industrial relations system and the availability of a range of alternative employee relations approaches other than traditional industrial relations and partnership.

The Legacy of the Workplace Partnerships of the 1990s

What can we say has been the legacy of these pioneering partnership cases to the study and practice of industrial and employee relations in Ireland? In terms of scholarship, there have been some outstanding Irish studies of workplace partnership that we have cited which have contributed both to practitioner understanding of the dynamics of this voluntary form of management-union cooperation as well as to academic and theoretical debates. The evidence shows that partnership can deliver significant gains to employers, employees and trade unions. The evidence also shows that starting and sustaining partnership is not an easy matter and that many difficulties can and do arise. Our understanding of these dynamics has been greatly enhanced by the study of actual cases of partnership in Ireland.

Without doubt it can be stated that there is now available to employers and trade unions – should they choose to use it – a well-tested and approved model of organisational change that can, notwithstanding difficulties in sustaining it over time, deliver significant benefits to all parties. These pioneering cases have demonstrated to employers and trade unions that they are not imprisoned within the traditional 'arms length' adversarial model of industrial relations and that they can expand their scope of engagement to issues outside the traditional bargaining agenda such as organisational change and improvement. They can expand, within the current adversarial model, their methods of engagement beyond traditional bargaining into joint consultation and joint problem solving. Unionised companies with a highly developed capacity for organisational change are likely to have, among other systems and procedures for harnessing workforce commitment, a partnership approach to employee relations based on openness and trust between management, employees and representatives (IBEC, 2008).

Workplace partnership has also provided a model of joint working that can be used within current adversarial arrangements without any formal adoption of partnership on an ongoing basis. We have seen that the LRC sponsors joint working parties on specific issues where parties require more time, information, external expertise and a wider range of options than is likely to arise in a traditional negotiation. There is, for example, anecdotal evidence of the use of joint working parties to review and amend company pension schemes. The deployment of external facilitators to help parties to define problems and to work towards their own solutions using a 'process consultation' approach has probably become more common in such cases, again largely because the role of facilitation has become familiar to industrial relations practitioners through its role in developing partnerships (Kessler and Purcell, 1994; Schein, 1999).

Terms and practices such as 'consensus decision-making', 'joint problem solving' and 'interest-based bargaining' that were exotic in the late 1990s are now much more familiar to many industrial relations practitioners as a consequence of their use in partnership. In this sense, the management and union 'toolkit' has been greatly enhanced as a consequence of these pioneering cases. Sometimes interest-based approaches to negotiations can best be developed within wider institutional innovations such as enterprise partnerships (IBEC, 2008).

Finally, it does not seem far-fetched to suggest that the introduction of alternative dispute resolution or 'ADR' including interest-based negotiation, fact-finding and other innovative means of resolving workplace disputes was facilitated by workplace partnership and its opening of management and trade union awareness to new ways of working together to solve common problems (Barrett and O'Dowd, 2005; IBEC, 2008).

Future Prospects

We have already seen that employers are more likely to behave in a short-term way based on immediate circumstances rather than on longer-term factors such as values or policy (Bacon and Storey, 2000: 423; Godard, 1997). In today's economic climate the emphasis is on short-term business goals and many manufacturing firms in particular are reducing staffing levels. In this context it seems that employers and trade unions are more likely to adopt power-based strategies in pursuit of their separate interests. There is some evidence from specialist publications such as *Industrial Relations News* that employers are seeking to redefine what constitutes 'good industrial relations' with more employers only offering statutory levels of redundancy payments and others choosing not to use the services of the LRC and Labour Court. There is evidence of employers taking a strong 'forcing' approach to organisational change aimed at quick achievement of reductions in pay and conditions of employment or staffing levels. These employers appear willing to accept that this 'forcing' approach will bring collateral damage to employment relations but seem prepared to endure this in order to achieve their immediate goals.

While most employers and trade unions are likely to remain within established norms of 'good industrial relations', it seems reasonable to conclude that in the current business climate employers are not likely to see partnership as providing speedy solutions to urgent problems including cost-cutting and restructuring. Where serious issues cannot be resolved at workplace level or through third party machinery, trade unions are more likely to initiate industrial action and perhaps even occupations or 'sit-ins' rather that to proposed closer engagement with employers through partnership. It has, doubtless, not been lost on trade unions that while partnership may have afforded them an enhanced role at workplace level as well as improved conditions of employment, it has not delivered the job security that is prized so much. While Government, IBEC and ICTU appear to remain committed at policy level to a 'single guiding vision' for employment relations at workplace level based on partnership principles, the practice on the ground does not reflect this guiding vision.

If it continues to be the case – as it was in our partnership cases – that employers find established collective bargaining arrangements satisfactory for handling mainstream industrial relations issues but unsatisfactory for handling organisational change, then it follows that certain employers will seek to handle organisational change outside industrial relations channels. In the current climate this seems more likely to lead them to unilateral decision-making and to forcing changes through than into joint decision-making and change through partnership.

Employers in Ireland have always insisted that partnership – and other forms of employee involvement – must be developed on a voluntary rather than a statutory basis and governments have refused to legislate other than on the basis of consensus between the social partners. Fear of frightening away direct foreign investment has been frequently cited as a key reason why governments would tread softly on issues such as trade union recognition and extended roles for trade unions at workplace level. Trade unions more or less lost the argument on the transposition into Irish law of the EU Directive on Information and Consultation. Short of further EU-wide initiatives there is little prospect of statutory forms of employee and trade union involvement being introduced.

We saw the importance of social partnership at national level for the development of partnership at workplace level. At the time of writing it is not clear if there is a future at least in the short term for national agreements of the 1987-2009 type. Even if there is to be a new agreement in 2009/2010, the overwhelming likelihood must be that the negotiation priorities of the parties will not include further initiatives around voluntary forms of employee and trade union involvement. Employer priorities are clearly fixed around competitiveness, costs and business restructuring. Trade union priorities in the private sector are clearly fixed around protecting jobs and wages including the national minimum wage, registered employment agreements and other wage-fixing mechanisms, and preventing what trade unions call the 'race to the bottom'. Achieving recognition at workplace level is likely to be of greater importance in coming years to trade unions than achieving a role as 'partners' in workplace let alone strategic-level decision-making. It needs to be remembered that trade unions were the driving force behind the development of workplace partnership through national agreements including the seminal *Partnership 2000*. It is worth noting how little emphasis there is today in industrial relations discourse on the common interests of employers, employees and trade unions in the private sector. National employer and trade union leaders tend to emphasise the importance of partnership at national level but to remain silent on partnership at workplace level.

This does not preclude the development of further partnership cases. As competitive pressures intensify it might well happen that employers and unions will see a logic in 'circling the wagons' through local partnership arrangements in order to ensure competiveness and to protect employment. Nor does it preclude employers and unions adopting partnership as a planned approach to future organisational changes. We have seen that employers will adopt partnership on the basis of a practical acceptance that it will help them to achieve the potential gains of changes that require the co-operation of employees and trade unions (Regini, 1995: 109). It is worth recalling the research finding that the issues of most concern to union members are not confined to the traditional industrial relations agenda but extend to working in co-operation with management in order to secure the future of their organisations (Geary, 2006). However, it is also worth recalling that union members appear to want their unions to play both co-operative and adversarial roles at once, the former on issues not covered by collective bargaining such as work organisation and the latter on pay and conditions (Eaton et al., 1992; Geary, 2006).

The overwhelming likelihood must, however, be that new partnership arrangements will be driven by local and pragmatic considerations and not by any overarching employer or trade union belief in the desirability of such arrangements or by dint of public policy. And it must also be likely that such developments will be isolated, small in number and arising in very specific sets of circumstances.

In light of these findings it seems reasonable to abandon as unrealistic the idea that partnership might become the dominant model of employee relations and organisational change in the unionised sector in Ireland. It makes far more sense to acknowledge the reality that industrial relations approaches will differ between organisations and sectors and that the pattern of 'fragmentation' is likely to endure rather than to cease.

Appendix

METHODOLOGY

'Voluntary' Forms of Workplace Partnership

By 'voluntary' we meant that a decision was taken by management and unions within a particular organisation to adopt a partnership approach to the handling of issues of mutual concern in general or of certain specific issues. The form of partnership could involve one group or committee or many; it could involve a single issue or many; but it had to involve some structure or process that was separate from collective bargaining and that involved either union representatives or staff members nominated with the consent of their trade unions. We excluded organisations that were not unionised because the international literature focussed almost exclusively on unionised organisations and because workplace partnership in Ireland was developed principally for application in such organisations.

We did not consider that most public service partnerships were 'voluntary' in our meaning of the term because in most cases their genesis lay in national and sectoral agreements to establish formal partnership structures rather than in local decisions made by management and unions. We considered this an important distinction to make on two grounds. Firstly, the theoretical literature upon which we were going to base our own research was grounded for the most part in 'voluntary' partnerships in the private sector. Secondly, public service partnerships were, in the main, only getting started when the research was being conducted and we did not consider that it would be possible to study how they worked and what their outcomes were in such circumstances. A small number of public service partnerships were included where it was evident that they had been established through local decisions in advance of the national and sectoral agreements.

Developing a List of All Known Cases

An initial part of the research involved the compilation of a listing of all known cases of 'voluntary' forms of workplace partnership in unionised organisations in Ireland.

The sources used to compile the list were: direct personal knowledge of the organisations or initiatives concerned; key informants among industrial relations practitioners such as personnel officers and trade union officials; contacts in national organisations such as the Irish Business and Employers' Confederation, the Irish Congress of Trade Unions and the then National Centre for Partnership; consultants and facilitators working in the partnership area; academic colleagues; the specialist journal *Industrial Relations News*; and other relevant publications including trade union journals, conference programmes, brochures and reports.

The initial intention was to use the list as a basis for a small number of case studies but as the list grew it became apparent that it could be used for a survey aimed at establishing the main features of each of the cases. In early 2000 we tested the list of partnership cases (which had grown to about two hundred initiatives) against the knowledge of some key informants. These were senior trade union and management executives with national responsibilities and pivotal roles in the development of partnership in companies. The responses indicated that this listing was comprehensive in that none of these key informants could add significantly to it. It was reasonable to have confidence, therefore, that the list constituted as accurate a list as could be compiled at that stage of all known cases of partnership then current. Given the smallness of Ireland and the centralisation of knowledge about industrial relations developments it was also reasonable to conclude at this stage that it was very unlikely that such informants would be unaware of cases of partnership to any significant degree. It was evident that the list represented a unique piece of research in itself and that it could be also be used for more detailed research. The final list of 143 cases could confidently be said to represent a very complete inventory of partnership initiatives in being at the time the survey was undertaken.

Unit of Analysis

The unit of analysis was the partnership in an organisation, whether this covered the entire organisation or a part thereof.

Survey Questionnaire

The survey took the form of a twelve-page questionnaire in booklet form and was organised under three main headings: the antecedents to the decision to establish partnership, the dynamics or institutional features of partnership in terms of structures and agendas, and the outcomes.

Management and Trade Union Participation in Questionnaire

Given that the partnership cases involved both management and trade unions in each organisation there was a strong argument for seeking to establish both a management and a trade union perspective on key issues such as reasons for establishment of partnership, assessment of relationships prior to the establishment of partnership and perception of outcomes (Cooke, 1990). It was difficult and time-consuming to compile an up-to-date register of the names and addresses of management recipients and it proved impractical to replicate such a list for trade union representatives.

The vast majority of the organisations on the list would have had more than one trade union and many would have had more than two. The trade unions concerned indicated to us that they could not provide from any central source the names and addresses of local representatives who were involved in the partnership cases in question. Furthermore, had it been possible to put together such a list within a reasonably quick time there could be no certainty of getting completed returns from both the management and union sides in any particular case or of getting all trade union recipients in any given organisation to respond. Given the emphasis in the literature on employer strategic choice in regard to HR/IR strategy development we decided that it would be legitimate to confine a survey of this type to a management perspective provided that the data analysis and conclusions took account of this. In the circumstances, therefore, we decided on both practical and theoretical grounds to focus the survey on managers only and to select the most senior personnel manager as the person to complete the questionnaire.

Response Rate

Given the small size of the population being surveyed it was going to be necessary to achieve a very high response rate in order to have sufficiently high quantity and quality data for analysis. At the same time, the size and complexity of the questionnaire was going to be a significant barrier to completion and return. For these reasons we decided early on to ask a number of individuals who would be better known personally to many respondents than the researcher to act as 'sponsors'. The role of sponsors was to select from the list any individuals personally known to them and to contact them either by letter, telephone or both in order to ask them to respond to the questionnaire. In this way we expected that potential respondents would complete the survey in order to oblige the sponsor and not just the researcher. We did not have sponsors for all the organisations on the list but we were in a position to rely on our own contacts in quite a number of cases.

The two sponsors who contacted most organisations were associated with the Labour Relations Commission and the former Irish Productivity Centre. This raises the possibility of a response bias towards organisations more prone to use the services of LRC and IPC but such organisations are more likely to be developing partnership anyway as a response to poor industrial relations or to the management of changes requiring the consent of trade unions and employees. For example, a number of cases appeared on the list because of reported recommendations to develop partnership emanating from the LRC or Labour Court or because of their involvement in IPC-funded partnership projects.

We received 96 responses in total. However, we eliminated companies from the original list as it became apparent that they should not have been on it in the first instance and we also eliminated public service organisations as we found out that the respondent organisations did not have voluntary partnerships as we had defined it. When the remaining 88 responses are calculated against the list of 143 cases the response rate becomes 62 per cent in rounded figures. This is a very satisfactory response rate for a postal survey of this kind, survey, and means that the sample can be viewed as representative of the survey population.

Numbers of Cases Used in Analysis

In Chapters 4, 5, and 6 we used data from all 88 cases. In Chapter 7 we reduced the number of cases to 78 because in ten cases there were details missing in respect to some key variables such as partnership structures which rendered problematical the allocation of these cases to one of our four types. Notwithstanding the fact that this research is of an exploratory kind, the small numbers mean that the statistical tests need to be treated with caution. Tests of levels of significance are based on $p < .10$, in other words we were willing to run a 1 in 10 chance that the reported relation-ships between variables could be due to chance rather than the existence of a real relationship between the variables in question. Often, however, the level of risk was lower, comprising a 5 in 100 risk or even 1 in 100 risk or lower. We are also using 'one-tailed' t-tests since we typically had clear expectations as to the direction of association between pairs of variables.

Operationalisation of the Four Partnership Types

The first step was to separate cases based on partnership struc-tures. The measures used to gather data relating to structures were yes/no questions relating to the presence of strategic and op-erational partnership bodies and the numbers of such bodies, the levels at which they operated, their titles, and institutional details such as membership, frequency and duration of meetings etc. A review of the survey responses showed that in 37 cases there were either strategic or operational bodies only. Thirty cases had opera-tional bodies only and the remaining 7 had strategic bodies only. In 42 cases there were both strategic and operational bodies. In 9 additional cases there was insufficient detailed information about structures to warrant inclusion in this part of the analysis but suf-ficient to have been included in the earlier descriptive chapters.

The second step was to decide how to divide the respondents into cases that had a 'weighty' 'mainstream' agenda and cases that had a 'light' 'mainstream' agenda. The principal measures used to gather data relating to partnership agendas were questions asking respondents to tick from a list of items presented to them the ones that had been discussed in the past six months at strategic and operational partnership bodies and, where appropriate, to list fur-ther items under an 'other' category. The bulk of the agenda items offered to survey respondents were designed to fit into a 'main-stream' definition, i.e. encompassing a range of issues that might broadly be described as 'soft' and 'hard' and relating to workplace relationships, business issues and industrial relations issues.

Given the types of agenda items considered 'mainstream' within the literature it appeared reasonable to consider most of the operational agenda items offered in the survey as 'mainstream' with the exception of social and recreational activities and facilities, canteen facilities and services, and fringe benefits such as holiday concessions and medical services. These might arguably be considered as typifying the early 'soft' QWL agendas and they have been omitted in order to strengthen the 'mainstream' character of the lists. It also seems reasonable to consider all of the strategic agenda items offered in the survey instrument as 'mainstream' without exception. See table below.

Table A1: Operational and Strategic Partnership Agendas

Operational Agenda 23 Items	Strategic Agenda 20 Items
Pay systems	Pay systems
Grading systems	Grading systems
Gain sharing	Gain sharing
New products/services	New products or services
Work practices	Strategic training plans
New technology/machinery	Cost savings
Workplace relations	Work practices
Business plans	New technology/machinery
New organisation structures	Staffing levels
Changes in ownership	Workplace relations
Financial performance	Business plans
IR grievances	New organization structures
Levels of customer service	Changes in ownership
Personnel and IR matters	Financial performance

Job security	Competitive position
Health and safety	Customer service
New forms of work organisation	Personnel and IR matters
Rosters and leave	New forms of work organisation
Equality issues	Job security
Communications	Health and safety systems
Staffing levels	
Cost savings	
Training	

Note: So few respondents used the 'other' categories to identify agenda items not provided for on the given lists that we do
not consider it worthwhile listing them here. Thus it appeared
reasonable to assume that the given items provided wide enough
scope for respondents to identify all the agenda items handled
through their strategic and operational partnership bodies.

In order to separate out cases based on the 'weight' of their
agendas it was decided to set a high qualifying measure of having
two-thirds of all the mainstream agenda items on the relevant recent partnership agendas. In cases where there were either strategic
or operational partnership bodies only this meant having two-
thirds or more of whichever agenda applied. In the case of strategic
bodies only this meant having 13 or more items or two thirds of 20
and in the case of operational bodies only it meant having 15 or
more items or two thirds of 23 items. In cases where there were
both strategic and operational bodies this meant having two-thirds
or more of the mainstream items on the combined strategic and operational partnership agendas, i.e. having 28 items or two thirds of
43 items. Using these decisions rules it was then possible to allocate
cases to each of the four types as set out in the Figure below.

Figure A1: Distributions of Cases into Four Types

Type 1: 'Exploratory' Partnerships	Type 3: 'Business' Partnerships
Mainly a Light Mainstream Agenda and Either Strategic or Operational Bodies	Mainly a Weighty Mainstream Agenda and Either Strategic or Operational Bodies
31 cases, 23 with operational bodies only and 8 with strategic bodies only	6 cases, 5 with operational bodies only and 1 with strategic bodies only
Type 2: 'Integrated Exploratory' Partnerships	Type 4: 'Integrated Business' Partnerships
Mainly a Light Mainstream Agenda and Both Strategic and Operational Bodies	Mainly a Weighty Mainstream Agenda and Both Strategic and Operational Bodies
32 cases	10 cases

There were 31 exploratory partnerships with an average of 7 agenda items each with a low of 3 and a high of 14. Five of these fell into a broadly 'commercial semi-state' category, 3 were public service organisations that had established partnership arrangements in advance of the rest of their sectors and the remaining 22 cases were private companies. Twenty-three of these partnerships had operational bodies only and 8 had strategic bodies only. The cases with operational bodies needed to have less than 13 agenda items to qualify for this type. In fact, the average number of agenda items for these cases was 8 items or 35 per cent of the possible total. The cases with strategic bodies needed to have less than 15 agenda items to qualify for this type. In fact, the average number of agenda items for these cases was 7 items or 35 per cent of the possible total.

There were 32 integrated exploratory partnerships cases with an average of 15 agenda items each with a low of 5 and a high of 22. Three of these integrated exploratory partnerships cases fell into a broadly 'commercial semi-state' category, six were public service organisations that had established partnership arrangements in advance of the rest of their sectors and the remaining 23 cases were private companies. All of these cases had to have both strategic and operational partnership bodies. To qualify for entry to this type cases had to have less than 29 agenda items from among the combined strategic and operational partnership agendas. The average number of agenda items was 15 or 35 per cent of the possible total.

There were 6 business partnerships with an average of 16 agenda items each with a low of 13 and a high of 18. Six out of the 7 cases were private companies and the other was a commercial state company. These cases could have either strategic or operational partnership bodies but all had operational bodies only except for one case. Cases with operational bodies only were required to have more than two thirds of the 23 mainstream items on the operational partnership agenda, i.e. more than 15. The average number of agenda items was 16 or 70 per cent of the possible total. The one case with strategic bodies only had 14 items, more than the required 13 or two thirds of the 20 items on the strategic agenda.

There were 10 integrated business partnerships with an average of 31 agenda items each with a low of 28 and a high of 36. Three of these were 'commercial semi-state' companies and the remaining 7 were private companies. These cases had to have both strategic and operational partnership bodies. On this basis, they were required to have two thirds or more of the 43 mainstream items on the combined operational partnership agenda, i.e. 28 or more. The average number of agenda items was 31 or 72 per cent of the possible total.

It is worth noting that both the business and integrated business partnership types had a higher percentage of possible agenda items than the exploratory and integrated exploratory types. It is also worth noting that there is a reasonably balanced distribution of cases in terms of having either strategic or operational partnership bodies only in 2000 – 37 cases – and having both strategic and operational partnership bodies – 42 cases.

On the other hand, only 16 cases or slightly more than 20 per cent had weighty mainstream agendas in 2000 as opposed to 63 or slightly less than 80 per cent that had light mainstream agendas. This is not surprising given that it has been seen from the literature review that employers and trade unions are unlikely to want to tackle significant change issues through what is frequently an untried and untested alternative to collective bargaining and managerial decision making in the absence of powerful external and internal pressures to do so. We know from Chapter 4 that the most commonly cited reason for adopting partnership was the anticipation of future significant changes rather than immediate economic or industrial relations crises.

Some specific cases might appear intuitively to be misplaced. A number of semi-state or privatised companies might be expected to have fitted into the integrated business partnership type with its weighty mainstream agenda and strategic and operational partnership bodies rather than into the integrated exploratory partnership type with its light mainstream agenda and combined strategic and operational partnership bodies. The most likely explanation is that at the time the survey was carried out that these cases were less advanced than they subsequently seem to have become. In the case of one privatised former utility the local partnership structures were only a short while in place at the time of surveying and many of the main elements of the 'transformation agreement' had been negotiated through a combination of collective bargaining and working parties in advance of the establishment of the wider partnership structures. Partnership in a public service commercial company was at an even earlier stage of development when the survey was conducted and partnership in a second utility has always been a second channel to industrial relations as far as the handling of significant organisational changes is concerned.

On the other hand, the partnerships in a number of other utilities appear to have weakened over the same period of time such that the main forms of decision making appear to now hinge around managerial prerogative and adversarial industrial relations with partnership confined very much to a 'backstage' role. Again, it is not surprising that some cases would advance and deepen while others would retreat and weaken given what is known from the international literature about the dynamic nature of voluntary forms of partnership and the manner in which changing environments can shift the emphasis in the employer agenda as well as the balance of relative power between trade unions and employers (Cooke, 1990).

These observations point to the fact that the allocation of cases to types is by way of being a 'snapshot' in time rather than a statement about the enduring character of any or all cases. For the purposes of the current research the allocations appear acceptable and to represent a reasonable basis for testing our assumptions relating to antecedents and types and to types and outcomes.

Note on Cluster Analysis Used in Chapter 7

Cluster analysis is an exploratory data analysis tool that can sort cases into groups such that the degree of association between cases is maximal if they belong to the same group and minimal otherwise. K-means cluster analysis may be used when a researcher already has hypotheses concerning the number of clusters in the cases or variables. In the present research we proposed that there were two broad sets of circumstances that might lead to the development of two different types of partnerships. We, therefore, formed two clusters that were as distinct as possible using the k-means clustering algorithm in SPSS. By examining the means on the different variables that we chose to form the clusters we profiled the clusters and explored our assumptions relating to possible influences of different sets of circumstances on the emergence of the two partnership types, i.e. 'exploratory' and 'business' partnerships. For reasons of presentation we simplified the cluster table in the text and we present the complete table here.

Table: Final Cluster Centres: Important Reasons for Adopting Partnership and Industrial Relations Characteristics

Variables	F	Chi	Cluster	
			1	2
Serious commercial difficulties necessitated significant changes for which we required the support of the workforce	39.493	.000	3.77	2.18
Very poor relationships with unions and workforce and we wanted to find ways of improving them	44.603	.000	3.43	1.91
Anticipated significant future changes in our commercial situation and we wanted to prepare the organisation for this	21.216	.000	4.14	3.12
Anticipated the need for further investment and could only obtain this on basis of major changes in management-union relations and work practices	30.746	.000	4	2
Experimenting with partnership to see what benefits it might bring	.948	.333	2.27	2.55
Degree of trade union involvement on a day-to-day basis	16.611	.000	3	2
Level of support for partnership among top management	5.246	.025	4	4
Level of support for partnership among full-time union officials	.004	.950	4	4
			57.14%	42.86%

The first five variables are coded as follows: 1=not important; 2=of some little importance; 3=important; 4=very important; 5-extremely important. The next five variables are coded as follows: 1=very low; 2=low; 3=moderate; 4=high; 5=very high.

Note on Regression Analysis Used in Chapter 7

In order to explore relationships between the different types of partnership arrangements and their outcomes we used ordinary least squares (OLS) regression analysis. OLS is an appropriate estimation method because this aspect of our research was exploratory and our dependent variables generally have an acceptable number of categories for OLS estimation (5-point ordinal scales). Regression analysis also allows us to explore the effects of variables that are categorical, such as our partnership types, by creating so-called 'dummy variables' that are coded either as a 1 or 0 and to then explore the relative effects of these variables on our outcomes variables. If a categorical variable such as a set of partnership types has x categories then the procedure requires us to create x-1 dummy variables. One type is then defined as the 'reference category' and the effects of other types are estimated with respect to this category or type.

Before exploring types and outcomes using regressions, we explored the possibility of factors such as organisation size, sector and ownership being associated with the outcomes. If they were shown to be, it would be necessary to include them in regressions as so-called 'control variables' to avoid their association with outcomes being spuriously attributed to the partnership types. To do this we ran regressions that included as independent variables a set of contextual variables only: large organisations with smaller organisations as the reference category; manufacturing with non-manufacturing as the reference category; and foreign-owned companies with non foreign-owned as the reference category. We followed this procedure because of the small sample size, because of the exploratory nature of the research and because it seemed best to test separately for possible control variable effects with a view to including these in the regressions containing partnership types only if their effects were confirmed. Including them in such a situation only would preclude otherwise insignificant control variables from masking the effects of partnership types on outcomes. If the controls had no effects then it would make sense to exclude them from the regressions containing partnership types. We included the control variables in regressions for all twenty-six current and future outcomes.

In the case of organisation size, having more than 250 employees had significant effects on three out of the 22 current outcomes variables included (all being significant at <0.1) and on none of the 22 future outcomes variables. In the case of sector, manufacturing had significant effects on four out of the 22 current outcomes variables included (three being significant at <0.1 and one at <0.05) and on four of the 22 future outcomes variables (three being significant at <0.05 and one at <0.1). In the case of ownership, foreign-owned had significant effects on five out of the 22 current outcomes variables included (two being significant at <0.05 and two at <0.1) and on three of the 22 future outcomes variables (one being significant at <0.1, one at <0.05 and one at <0.01). The control variables appeared to have somewhat more influence on outcomes of particular importance to employees than on outcomes of particular importance to management and trade unions. On the basis that these control variables only appeared to have significant effects in the case of 18 out of a total of 132 outcomes variables, we considered it reasonable to exclude them from the regressions used to explore relationships between our partnership types as independent variables and the outcomes as dependent variables.

Limitations of Research

Certain limitations of the research that have already been flagged in the text need to be restated and commented on here. We have accepted that our sample size was small. However, the population was also small and the response rate was satisfactory. In addition, we were satisfied that our survey was based on the most accurate listing of extant cases of workplace partnership that it was possible to compile at that time.

The same respondents provided the descriptive data on the partnerships and the judgments on the effects of these partnerships, thus introducing the possibility of 'common method bias'. It is conceivable that respondents who were less closely associated with the subject of the research might have given less positive reports. It was not considered feasible to collect data on outcomes from a separate source and in any event it was not clear that other respondents would be better placed to provide more accurate information on outcomes.

As already stated, we had no employee or trade union input to the surveys. So we had to rely on management respondents to give judgments on the effects of partnership on employees and trade unions. It is possible that employee and trade union respondents would have given different judgments on outcomes. However, we considered it reasonable to confine the survey to managers on both practical and theoretical grounds. The exclusion of union respondents is an obvious limitation of the study, and we make no claim that management views regarding outcomes examined correlate with the views of union officials or employees.

In addition, the partnerships that we surveyed were mostly of quite recent provenance. Many were operational for only two to three few years and several for even shorter periods. Other researchers have limited the involvement of companies to those with partnerships that were at least four years old (Cooke, 1990). We sought to overcome this weakness by asking questions about expected future outcomes in addition to the questions on current outcomes.

We have also noted that the design of our questionnaire may have had some weaknesses. For example, we suggested in Chapter 7 that our definitions of agendas as 'light' and 'weighty' might not have captured adequately critical differences between agendas. Consequently, more complex or different questions may be needed in future research around these areas. In addition, we limited responses on agendas to the ticking of boxes on issues that had been on the agenda and to identifying the most important items on the lists. We did not ask questions about what had happened to the agenda items such as whether or not they were still on the agenda, had been agreed or disagreed or if changes had been implemented on foot of these items being on the partnership agenda. It is arguable that probing for such details would have proved impossible in a survey of this type and that such detail might best be established through other research approaches such as in-depth case studies.

Finally, there is the possibility that surveys of this type might, in themselves, limit the types of findings and conclusions that can be reached on complex and highly 'processual' phenomena such as workplace partnership. For example, some of our findings such as why a slight majority of our 'exploratory' partnerships appeared in identical circumstances to our business partnerships might best be explained by 'process' aspects of partnership that we had not included in the survey such as leadership. We suggested that it was not possible to adequately measure such in a survey of this type.

BIBLIOGRAPHY

Government Publications

(All published by the Government Publications Office, Dublin)

Department of Enterprise Trade and Employment (2008): *S.I. No. 132 of 2008 Industrial Relations Act 1990 (Code of Practice on Information and Consultation (Declaration) Order 2008*, Dublin: Stationery Office.

Department of Labour (1986): *Report of the Advisory Committee on Worker Participation*, Dublin: Stationery Office.

Government of Ireland (1991): *Programme for Economic and Social Progress*, Dublin: Stationery Office.

Government of Ireland (1994*): Programme for Competitiveness and Work*, Dublin: Stationery Office.

Government of Ireland (1997): *Partnership 2000*, Dublin: Stationery Office.

Government of Ireland (2000): Programme *for Prosperity and Fairness*, Dublin: Stationery Office.

Government of Ireland (2003): *Sustaining Progress*, Dublin: Stationery Office.

Government of Ireland (2006): *Towards 2016: Ten-Year Framework Social Partnership Agreement 2006-2015*, Dublin: Stationery Office.

Government of Ireland (2008): *Towards 2016 Draft Transitional Agreement Pay and the Workplace*, Dublin: Stationery Office.

Reports

Cahill, N. (2000): *Profit Sharing, Employee Share Ownership and Gainsharing: What Can They Achieve?* Dublin: NESC.

European Foundation for the Improvement of Living and Working Conditions (EFILWC) (1997): *New Forms of Work Organisation: Can Europe Realise its Potential?*, Dublin: EFILWC.

Forfas (1996): *Shaping Our Future: A Strategy for Enterprise in Ireland in the 21st Century*, Dublin: Forfas.

Healy, S. (2000): *The Partnership in Action at Enterprise Level Project: Independent Evaluation Report*, Dublin: IBEC/ICTU.

Health Service Executive (HSE)(2008): *Improving Our Services: A Users' Guide to Managing Change in the Health Service Executive*, Dublin: HSE.

Health Services National Partnership Forum (HSNPF) (2004): *Learning in Partnership: A Review of Health Services Partnership*, Dublin: HSNPF.

Human Resources Development Canada (HRDC) (1997): *Quebec Labour and Management Experiences with Workplace Innovation*, Montreal: HRDC.

Human Resources Development Canada (HRDC) (1998): *Evaluation of the Labour-Management Partnerships Programme*, Montreal: HRDC.

Irish Business and Employers' Confederation (IBEC) (1998): *Guidelines for the Development of Partnership in Competitive Enterprise*, Dublin: IBEC.

Irish Business and Employers' Confederation (IBEC) (2008): *The Essential Guide to Alternative Dispute Resolution: Innovative Approaches to Problem Solving and Dispute Resolution*, Dublin: IBEC.

Irish Business and Employers' Confederation (IBEC) (2008): *The Essential Guide to Change: A People-Centred Approach*, Dublin: IBEC.

Irish Congress of Trade Unions (ICTU) (1993): *New Forms of Work Organisation: Options for Unions*, Dublin: ICTU.

Irish Congress of Trade Unions (ICTU) (1995): *Managing Change: Review of Union Involvement in Company Restructuring*, Dublin: ICTU.

Irish Congress of Trade Unions (ICTU) (1997): *Partnership in the Workplace: Guidelines for Trade Unions*, Dublin: ICTU.

Irish Congress of Trade Unions (ICTU) (2008): *The Employees (Provision of Information and Consultation) Act 2006: A Guide to the New Information and Consultation Processes for Trade Unions*, Dublin: ICTU.

Irish Productivity Centre (IPC) (1986): *A Guide to Employee Shareholding through Profit Sharing*, Dublin: IPC.

Irish Productivity Centre (IPC) (1999): *ANORD Enterprise Level Case Study: The New Work Organisation in Ireland Programme, Partnership Development at Enterprise Level*, Dublin: IPC.

Knell, J. (1999): *Partnership at Work, Employment Relations Research Series No. 7*, London: Department of Trade and Industry.

Labour Relations Commission (LRC) (1996): *A Strategic Policy*, Dublin: LRC.

Lazes, P. (2001): *Partnership in Local Authorities*, Dublin: LANPAG.

Lazes, P. (2001): *Health Services National Partnership Reflection and Learning Report*, Dublin: HSNPF.

McAdam, J. (1999): *WRAPSA Mainstreaming Project: Report to Leargas*, Dublin: WRAPSA.

Murphy, T., and Walsh, D. (1980): *The Worker Director and his Impact on the Enterprise: Expectations, Experiences and Effectiveness in Seven Irish Companies: Summary Report*, Dublin: Irish Productivity Centre.

National Centre for Partnership and Performance (NCPP) (2002): *Modernising Our Workplaces for the Future: A Strategy for Change and Innovation*, Dublin: NCPP.

National Centre for Partnership and Performance (NCPP) (2003): *Achieving High Performance: Partnership Works – The International Evidence*, Dublin: NCPP.

National Centre for Partnership and Performance (NCPP) (2004a): *The Changing Workplace: A Survey of Employee's Views and Expectations*, Dublin: NCPP.

National Centre for Partnership and Performance (NCPP) (2004b): *The Changing Workplace: A Survey of Employers' Views and Expectations*, Dublin: NCPP.

National Centre for Partnership and Performance (NCPP) (2004c): *Information and Consultation: A Case Study Review of Current Practice*, Dublin: NCPP.

National Centre for Partnership and Performance (NCPP) (2005): *Working to our Advantage: A National Workplace Strategy*, Dublin: NCPP.

National Economic and Social Council (NESC) (1996): *Strategy Into the 21st Century*, Dublin: NESC.

National Economic and Social Council (NESC) (1999): *Opportunities, Challenges and Capacities for Choice*, Dublin: NESC.

O'Donnell, R. and O'Reardon, C. (2000): 'Social Partnership in Ireland's Economic Transformation' in G. Fajertag and P. Pochett (eds.), *Social Pacts in Europe – New Dynamics*, Brussels: ETUI.

O'Dwyer, J.J., O'Dowd, J., O'Halloran, J. and Cullinane, J. (2002): *Partnership in the Civil Service: A Formal Review*, Dublin: Department of Finance.

Services Industrial Professional Technical Union (SIPTU) (1999): *Participation and Partnership in Changing Work Organization*, Dublin: SIPTU.

Services Industrial Professional Technical Union (SIPTU) (2000): *Adapt Project Final Report: SIPTU Enterprise Partnership (CO 27)*, Dublin: SIPTU.

Totterdill, P. and Sharpe, A. (1999): *New Work Organisation in Ireland: Report of the Independent Evaluator*, Dublin: Irish Productivity Centre.

Worker Representatives as Proactive Stakeholders in Airlines (WRAPSA) (1998): *The WRAPSA Project: Report of the Project Steering Committee*, Dublin: SIPTU/Aer Lingus/ICTU.

Academic Theses

Eaton, A. (1988): *Local Union Control of Worker Participation and Labour-Management Cooperation Programmes*, University of Wisconsin.

Gormley, T. (2008): *Workplace Partnership in Context: The Effects of Industrial Relations Settings on Partnership Processes and Outcomes in the Case of the Irish State Broadcasting Authority (RTÉ)*, University College Dublin.

Hastings, T. (2001): *Marketisation and Industrial Relations in State Owned Companies: A Theoretical and Empirical Study of Change Initiatives in Four Irish Commercial Semi-State Companies*, University College Dublin.

Rosen, M. (1998): *The A.O. Smith Corporation and AFL-CIO Directly Affiliated Local 19806: A Study of Labour-Management Co-operation in the Era of Globalization and Lean Production*, University of Wisconsin-Milwaukee.

Wall, T. (2004): *Understanding Irish Social Partnership: An Assessment of Competitive Corporatist and Post-Corporatist Perspectives*, University College Dublin.

Books and Articles

Allen, K. (2000): *The Celtic Tiger: The Myth of Social Partnership in Ireland*, Manchester: Manchester University Press.

Amis, J., Slack, T. and Hinings, C.R. (2002): 'Values and Organizational Change', *The Journal of Applied Behavioural Science*, Vol. 38, No. 4: 436-66.

Applebaum, E., Bailey, T., Berg, P., Kalleberg, A.L. (2000): *Manufacturing Advantage: Why High Performance Work Systems Pay Off*, London: Cornell University Press.

Bacon, N. and Storey, J. (2000): 'New Employee Relations Strategies in Britain: Towards Individualism or Partnership?', *British Journal of Industrial Relations*, Vol. 38, No. 3, 407-427.

Baglioni, G. and Crouch, C. (1992): *European Industrial Relations: The Challenge of Flexibility*, London: Sage.

Barling, J., Fullage, C., and Kelloway, K.E. (1992): *The Union and Its Members: A Psychological Approach*, New York: Oxford University Press.

Barrett, J.T. and O'Dowd, J. (2005): *Interest-Based Bargaining: A Users Guide*, Trevet Grange: OD Books in association with Trafford Publishing.

Batt, R. and Appelbaum, E. (1995): 'Worker Participation in Diverse Settings: Does the Form Affect the Outcome, and If So Who Benefits?' *British Journal of Industrial Relations*, Vol. 33, No. 3: 353-378.

Bean, R. (1994): *Comparative Industrial Relations: an introduction to cross-national perspectives*, London: Routledge.

Beckhard, R. and Harris, D. (1977): *Organisation Transitions: Managing Complex Change*, Reading, MA: Addison-Wesley.

Black, S.E. and Lynch, L.M. (1997): 'How to Compete: The impact of workplace practices and information technology on productivity', National Bureau of Economic Research Working Paper No. 6120, Cambridge: MA.

Black, S.E. and Lynch, L.M. (2000): 'What's driving the new economy: The benefits of workplace innovation', National Bureau of Economic Research Working Paper No. 7479, Cambridge: MA.

Bushe, G.R. (1988): 'Developing Cooperative Labour-Management Relations in Unionized Factories: A Multi-Case Study of Quality Circles and Parallel Organisation within Joint QWL Projects', *Journal of Applied Behavioural Science*, Vol. 24: 129-150.

Clarke, L. and Haiven, L. (1999): 'Workplace Change and Continuous Bargaining: Saskatoon Chemicals Then and Now', *Relations Industriellles/ Industrial Relations, Vol.54: 168-193.*

Coghlan, D. and McAuliffe, E. (2003): *Changing Healthcare Organisations.* Dublin: Blackhall Publishing.

Cohen-Rosenthal, E. and Burton, C. (1987): *Mutual Gains: A Guide to Union-Management Co-operation,* New York: Praeger.

Cooke, W.N. (1990): *Labor-Management Cooperation: New Partnerships or Going Around in Circles*? Kalamazoo, Michigan, W.E. Upjohn Institute for Employment Research.

Cooke, W.N. (1992): 'Product Quality Improvement Through Employee Participation: The Effects of Unionization and Joint Union-Management Administration', *Industrial and Labour Relations Review,* Vol. 46, No. 1, 119-34.

Cooke, W.N. (1994): 'Employee Participation Programs, Group-Based Incentives, and Company Performance: A Union-Non Union Comparison', *Industrial and Labour Relations Review,* Vol. 47, No. 4.

Crouch, C. (1994): *Industrial Relations and European State Traditions,* Oxford: Clarendon Press.

Cully, M., Dix, G., O'Reilly, A. and Woodland, S. (1999): *Britain at Work: As Depicted by the 1998 Workplace Employee Relations Survey,* London: Routledge.

Cummins, T. (2009): 'Beating the Downturn: How AXA and Its Unions Manage Change', Presentation to Industrial Relations News Conference, Dublin, 5 March 2009.

Cutcher-Gershenfeld, J. (1991): 'The Impact on Economic Performance of a Transformation in Industrial Relations', *Industrial and Labour Relations Review,* Vol. 44, No. 2, 241-60.

Cutcher-Gershenfeld, J. and Verma, A. (1994): 'Joint Governance in North American Workplaces: A Glimpse of the Future or the End of an Era?', *International Journal of Human Resource Management,* Vol.5, No.3, 547-80.

Cradden, T. (1992): 'Trade Unionism and HRM: the Incompatibles?', *Irish Business and Administrative Research,* 13: 36-47.

D'Art, D. and Turner, T. (2002): 'An Attitudinal Revolution in Irish Industrial Relations: the End of 'Them and Us'?', in Daryl D'Art and Tom Turner (eds.) *Irish Employment Relations in the New Economy,* Dublin: Blackhall Publishing.

Danford, A., Richardson, M., Stewart, P., Tailby, S. and Upchurch, M. (2005): *Partnership and the High Performance Workplace: Work and Employment Relations in the Aerospace Industry,* London: Palgrave Macmillan.

Dawson, P. (1994): *Organisational Change: A Processual Approach,* London: Paul Chapman Publishing Ltd.

Deakin, S., Hobbs, R., Konzelmann, S.J. and Wilkinson, F. (2002): 'Partnership, Ownership and Control: The Impact of Corporate Governance on Employment Relations', *Employee Relations,* 24, 3: 335-51.

Deakin, S., Hobbs, R., Konzelmann, S.J. and Wilkinson, F. (2005): 'Working Corporations: Corporate Governance and Innovation' in 'Labour-Management Partnerships in Britain', M. Stuart and M. Martinez-Lucio (eds.), *Partnership and Modernization in Employment Relations,* Oxford: Routledge.

Deery, S.J. and Iverson, R.D. (2005): 'Labour-Management Cooperation: Antecedents and Impact on Organizational Performance', *Industrial and Labour Relations Review,* Vol. 58, No. 4: 588-609

Dobbins, T. (2008): *Workplace Partnership in Practice: Securing Mutual Gains at Waterford Glass and Aughinish Alumina?,* Dublin: The Liffey Press.

Dundon, T., Curran, D., Maloney, M. and Ryan, P. (2003): *Organisational Change and Employee Information and Consultation,* CISC Working Paper No. 12, Centre for Innovation and Structural Change, National University of Ireland, Galway.

Dundon, T., Curran, D., Maloney, M. and Ryan, P. (2008): *The Transposition of the European Employee Information and Consultation Directive Regulations in the Republic of Ireland*, CISC Working Paper No. 26, Centre for Innovation and Structural Change, National University of Ireland, Galway.

Eaton, A.E., Gordon, M.E., and Keefe, J.H. (1992): 'The Impact of Quality of Work Life Programmes and Grievance System Effectiveness on Union Commitment', *Industrial and Labour Relations Review*, Vol. 45, No. 3, 591-04.

Eaton, A. E. (1994): 'The Survival of Employee Participation Programmes in Unionised Settings', *Industrial and Labour Relations Review*, Vol. 47, No. 3, 371-89.

Eaton, A.E., Rubinstein, S.A., Kochan, T.A. (2008): 'Balancing Acts: Dynamics of a Union Coalition in a Labour Management Partnership', *Industrial Relations*, Vol. 47, No. 1, 10-35.

Edwards, P., Belanger, J. and Haiven, L. (1994): 'The Workplace and Labour Relations in Comparative Perspective', in J. Belanger, P.K. Edwards and L. Haiven (eds.) *Workplace Industrial Relations and the Global Challenge*, Ithaca: ILR Press.

Edwards, P., Belanger, J. and Wright, M. (2002): 'The Social Relations of Productivity: A Longitudinal and Comparative Study of Aluminium Smelters', *Relations Industriellles/Industrial Relations*, Vol. 57, No. 2: 309-330.

Edwards, P., Collinson, M. and Rees, C. (1998): 'The Determinants of Employee Responses to Total Quality Management: Six Case Studies', *Organisation Studies*, Vol. 19, No. 3: 449-475.

Faulkner, M. (2007): *Essentials of Irish Labour Law*, Dublin: Gill and Macmillan.

Federation of Irish Employers (FIE)/Irish Congress of Trade Unions (ICTU) (1991): *Joint Declaration on Employee Involvement in the Private Sector*, Dublin: FIE/ICTU.

Fenton-O'Creevy, M. (1998): 'Employee Involvement and the Middle Manager: Evidence from a Survey of Organizations', *Journal of Organizational Behaviour*, Vol. 19: 67-84.

Ferner, F. and Hyman, R. (1994) (eds.): *New Frontiers in Industrial Relations*, Oxford: Blackwell.

Flanders, A. (1967): *Collective Bargaining: Prescriptions for Change*, London: Faber.

Freeman, R.B. and Rogers, J. (1999): *What Workers Want*, Cornell University Press.

Freeman, R.B. and Medoff, J.L. (1984): *What Do Unions Do?*, New York: Basic Books.

Freeman, R.B., Kleiner, M.M. and Ostroff, C. (2000): 'The Anatomy of Employee Involvement and its Effects on Firms and Workers', National Bureau of Economic Research Working Paper 805, MA: National Bureau of Economic Research.

Frohlich, D. and Pekruhl, U. (1996): *Direct Participation and Organisational Change: Fashionable but Misunderstood?, An analysis of recent research in Europe, Japan and the USA*, European Foundation for the Improvement of Living and Working Conditions, EF/96/38/EN.

Frost, A. C. (2000): 'Explaining Variation in Workplace Restructuring: The Role of Local Union Capabilities', *Industrial and Labour Relations Review*, Vol. 54, No. 4: 559–78.

Geary, J.F. (1999): 'The New Workplace: Change at Work in Ireland'. *International Journal of Human Resource Management*, 10 (5): 870-890.

Geary, J. (2006): 'Employee Voice in the Irish Workplace: Status and Prospect', in P. Boxall, P. Haynes and R. Freeman (eds.), *Employee Voice in the Anglo-American World*, Ithaca, NY: ILR Press.

Geary, J.F. and Roche, W.K. (2003): 'Workplace Partnership and the Displaced Activist Thesis', *Industrial Relations Journal*, Vol. 34: 32-51.

Geraghty, D. (1992): World Class Participation: The Seventh Countess Markievicz Lecture, Dublin: Irish Association for Industrial Relations.

Giles, A., Lapointe, P.A., Murray, G. and Belanger, J. (1999): 'Industrial Relations in the New Workplace', *Relations Industrielles/Industrial Relations*, Vol. 54, No. 1, 15-22.

Gill, C. and Krieger, H. (2000): 'Recent Survey Evidence on Participation in Europe: wards a European Model?' *European Journal of Industrial Relations*, 6(1): 109-32.

Gilson, C.H.J. and Wagar, T. (2000), 'Human resource management and labour management committees: From contracts to consultation?', *New Zealand Journal of Industrial Relations*, 25 (2): 169-181.

Gilvarry, E. and Hunt, B. (2008): 'Trade Union Recognition and the Labour Court: Picking up the Pieces after Ryanair', in T. Hastings (ed.), *The State of the Unions: Challenges Facing Organised Labour in Ireland*, Dublin: The Liffey Press.

Godard, J. (1997): 'Managerial Strategies, Labour and Employment Relations, and the State', *British Journal of Industrial Relations*, Vol. 35, No. 3, 399–426.

Goll, I. (1991): 'Environment, Corporate Ideology, and Employee Involvement Programmes', *Industrial Relations*, Vol. 30, No. 1: 138-149.

Goll, I. and Zeitz, G. (1991): 'Conceptualising and Measuring Corporate Ideology', *Organization Studies*, Vol. 12, No. 2: 191-207.

Grattan, J. (1997): 'Worker Democracy and Employee Involvement Plans' in B. Nissen (ed.): *Unions and Workplace Reorganization*, Michigan: Wayne State University Press.

Guest, D.E. and Peccei, R. (2001): 'Partnership at Work: Mutuality and the Balance of Advantage', *British Journal of Industrial Relations*, Vol. 39, No. 2.

Gunnigle, P. (1998): 'More Rhetoric than Reality: Enterprise Level Industrial Relations Partnerships in Ireland', *The Economic and Social Review*, Vo. 28, No. 4: 179-200.

Gunnigle, P. and Dobbins. T. (2009): 'Can Voluntary Workplace Partnership Deliver Sustainable Mutual Gains?' *British Journal of Industrial Relations*, Vol. 47, No. 3, 546–70.

Gunnigle, P., Flood, P, Morley, M. and Turner, T. (1994): *Continuity and Change in Irish Employee Relations*, Dublin: Oak Tree Press.

Gunnigle, P. and Roche, W.K. (1995): *New Challenges to Irish Industrial Relations*, Dublin: Oak Tree Press in association with the Labour Relations Commission.

Gunnigle, P., Morley, M., Clifford, N. and Turner, T. (1997) *Human Resource Management in Irish Organisations: Practice in Perspective*, Dublin: Oak Tree Press.

Hanlon, R. (1976): *Joint Consultation in Irish Industry*, Dublin: Irish Productivity Centre.

Hammer, T.H., Currall, S.C., and Stern, R.N. (1991): 'Worker Representation on Boards of Directors: A Study of Competing Roles', *Industrial and Labour Relations Review,* Vol. 44, No. 4, 661-80.

Hammer, T.H. and Stern, R.N. (1986): 'A Yo-Yo Model of Co-operation: Union Participation in Management at the Rath Packing Company', *Industrial and Labour Relations Review,* Vol. 39, No. 3, 337-49.

Harrison, D. and Laplante, N. (1996): 'TQM, Trade Unions and Cooperation: Case Studies in Quebec Manufacturing Plants', *Economic and Industrial Democracy,* Vol. 17: 99-129.

Hastings, T. (1994): *Semi-States in Crisis: The Challenge for Industrial Relations in the ESB and Other Major Semi-State Companies,* Dublin: Oak Tree Press.

Hastings, T. (2003): *Politics, Management and Industrial Relations: Semi-State Companies and the Challenges of Marketisation,* Dublin: Blackhall Publishing.

Hastings, T. (2008) (ed.): *The State of the Unions: Challenges Facing Organised Labour in Ireland,* Dublin: The Liffey Press.

Hastings, T., Sheehan, B. and Yeates, P. (2007): *Saving the Future: How Social Partnership Shaped Ireland's Economic Success,* Dublin: Blackhall Publishing.

Heaton, N., Mason, B. and Morgan, J. (2002): 'Partnership and Multi-Unionism in the Health Service', *Industrial Relations Journal,* 33, 2, 112-26.

Heckscher, C.C. (1988): *The New Unionism: Employee Involvement in the Changing Corporation,* New York: Basic Books.

Herrick, N.Q. (1985): 'Parallel Organizations in Unionized Settings: Implications for Organizational Research', *Human Relations,* Vol. 38, No. 10: 963-981.

Havlovic, S.J. (1991): 'Quality of Work Life and Human Resource Outcomes', *Industrial Relations,* Vol. 30, No. 3, 469-79.

Hodgkinson, A. (1999): *Employee Involvement and Participation in the Organizational Change Decision: Illawarra and Australian Patterns,* University of Wollongong Department of Economics Working Paper Series.

Hyman, J. and Mason, B. (1995), *Managing Employee Involvement and Participation,* London: SAGE.

Ichniowski, T., Kochan, T.A., Levine, D., Olson, C. and Strauss, G. (1996): 'What Works at Work: Overview and Assessment', *Industrial Relations*, Vol. 35, No. 3, 299-333.

Jacobson, D. (1996): 'New Forms of Work Organisation in Ireland: An Annotated Bibliography', Dublin City University Business School, Research Papers, No. 9.

Kaminski, M. (1997): 'The Union Role in the Team Concept: A Case Study', in Steve Babson and Huberto Juarez Nunez (eds.) *Confronting Change: Auto Workers and Lean Production in North America*, Detroit: Wayne State University Press.

Kaminski, M., Bertelli, D., Moye, M., and Yudken, J. (1996): *Making Change Happen: Six Cases of Unions and Companies Transforming Their Workplaces*, Washington D.C.: Work and Technology Institute.

Katz, H.C., Kochan, T.A. and Gobeille, K.R. (1983): 'Industrial Relations Performance, Economic Performance, and QWL Programmes: An Interplant Analysis', *Industrial and Labour Relations Review*, Vol. 37, No. 1, 3-17.

Katz, H.C. and Darbishire, O. (2000): *Converging Divergences: Worldwide Changes in Employment Systems*, Ithaca, NY: ILR Press.

Kelly, A. (1989): 'The Worker Director in Irish Industrial Relations' in *Industrial Relations in Ireland: Contemporary Issues and Developments*, Dublin: University College Dublin.

Kelly, A. and Hourihan, F. (1994): 'Employee Participation' in Murphy, T. and Roche, W.K. (eds.) *Irish Industrial Relations in Practice*, Dublin: Oak Tree Press.

Kelly, J. (1999): 'Social Partnership in Britain: Good for Profits, Bad for Jobs and Unions', *Communist Review*, Autumn.

Kelly, J. (2004): 'Social Partnership Agreements in Britain: Labour Cooperation and Compliance', *Industrial Relations*, Vol. 43, No 1: 267-392.

Kessler, I. and Purcell, J. (1994): 'Joint problem solving and the role of third parties: An evaluation of the ACAS advisory work', *Human Resource Management Journal*, Vol. 4 No.2, pp.1-21.

Kochan, T. A. and Dyer, L. (1976): 'A Model of Organisational Change in the Context of Labor-Management Relations', *Journal of Applied Behavioural Science*, Vol. 12, No. 2, pp 59-78.

Kochan, T.A., Katz, H.C. and Mower, N.R. (1984): *Worker Participation and American Unions: Threat or Opportunity?* Kalamazoo, Michigan, W.E. Upjohn Institute for Employment Research.

Kochan, T.A., Katz, H.C. and McKersie, R.B. (1989): *The Transformation of American Industrial Relations,* New York: Basic Books.

Kochan, T. and Osterman, P. (1994): *The Mutual Gains Enterprise,* Boston, MA, Harvard Business School Press.

Kumar, P. (2000): *Rethinking High-Performance Work Systems,* Current Issues Series, Kingston: Queen's University.

Kumar, P., Murray, G. and Schetagne, S. (1998): *Workplace Change in Canada: Union Perceptions of Impacts, Responses and Support Systems,* Current Issues Series, Kingston: Queen's University.

Lavelle, J., Gunnigle, P., and McDonnell, A. (2008): 'Unions on the Edge? Industrial Relations in Multinational Companies', in T. Hastings (ed.): *The State of the Unions: Challenges Facing Organised Labour in Ireland,* Dublin: The Liffey Press.

Lazes, P. and Savage. J. (1997): 'New Unionism and the Workplace of the Future', in B. Nissen, (ed.): *Unions and Workplace Reorganization, Michigan:* Wayne State University Press.

Levine, D.I. (1995): *Reinventing the Workplace: How Business and Employees Can Both Win,* Washington: The Brookings Institution.

Lloyd, C. and Newell, H. (2001): 'Changing Management-Union Relations: Consultation in the UK Pharmaceutical Industry', *Economic and Industrial Democracy,* Vol. 22: 357-382.

Locke, R., Kochan, T., and Piore, M. (1995) (eds.): *Employment Relations in a Changing World Economy,* Cambridge: MIT Press.

Marchington, M. (1992): *The Practice of Joint Consultation in Australia – A Preliminary Analysis of the AWIRS Data,* ACIRRT Working Paper No. 21, University of Sydney Australian Centre for Industrial Relations Research and Teaching.

Marchington, M., Wilkinson, A., Ackers, P., and Goodman, J. (1994): 'Understanding the Meaning of Participation: Views from the Workplace', *Human Relations,* Vol. 47, No. 8, pp 867-93.

Marchington, M., Wilkinson, A., Ackers, P., and Dundon, T. (2001): *Management Choice and Employee Voice*, London: Chartered Institute of Personnel and Development.

Marks, A., Findlay, P., Hine, J., McKinlay, A. and Thompson, P. (1998): 'The Politics of Partnership? Innovation in Employment Relations in the Scottish Spirits Industry', *British Journal of Industrial Relations*, Vol. 36, No. 2: 209-26.

McCarthy, C. (1975): 'Worker Participation in Ireland: Problems and Strategies', *Administration*, 23(2): 10-9.

McCartney, J. and Teague, P. (1997): 'Workplace Innovation in the Republic of Ireland', *The Economic and Social Review*, Vol. 28, No. 2: 158-170.

Mc Kersie, R.B. (2002): 'Labour-Management Partnerships: US Evidence and Implications for Ireland', in P. Gunnigle, M. Morley and M. McDonnell (eds.) *The John Lovett Lectures: A Decade of Developments in Human Resource Management*, Dublin: The Liffey Press.

Merrigan, M. (2007): 'Finding Common Ground' in Eilish McAuliffe and Kenneth McKenzie (eds.), *The Politics of Healthcare*, Dublin: The Liffey Press.

Millward, N., Stevens, M., Smart, D. and Hawes, W.R. (1992): *Workplace Industrial Relations in Transition,* Aldershot: Dartmouth Publishing Company.

Mooney, P. (2005): *Union-Free: Creating a Committed and Productive Workforce*, Dublin: The Liffey Press.

Mulvey, C. (1972): *Industrial Democracy: Forms of Employee Representation in Industrial Relations*, Dublin: Federated Union of Employers and Confederation of Irish Industry.

Murphy T.V. and Roche, W.K. (1994): *Irish Industrial Relations in Practice,* Dublin: Oak Tree Press in association with Graduate School of Business University College Dublin.

Neumann, J.E., Holti, R. and Standing, H. (1995): *Change Everything at Once: The Tavistock Institute's Guide to Developing Teamwork in Manufacturing*, Oxfordshire: Management Books 2000 Ltd.

O'Dowd, J. (1998): *Employee Partnership in Ireland: A Guide for Managers,* Dublin: Oak Tree Press.

O'Dowd, J. (1999): 'Industrial Relations Partnership at the Level of the Workplace', in P. Gunnigle (ed.), *The Irish Employee Recruitment Handbook*, Dublin: Oak Tree Press.

O'Dowd, J. (2002): 'If It Ain't Broke – Fix It Anyway: How Partnership Can Help Improve Industrial Relations', *LRC Journal*, Vol. 1.

O'Dowd, J. and Roche, W.K. (2009): 'Partnership Structures and Agendas and Managers' Assessments of Stakeholder Outcomes', *Industrial Relations Journal*, Vol. 40, 1, 17-39.

O'Kelly, K. (1995): 'Ireland: A Joint Approach to Direct Participation in I. Regalia and C. Gill (eds.) *The Position of the Social Partners in Europe on Direct Participation, Country Studies,* Vol. 1, Working Paper No. WP/95/35/EN, Dublin: European Foundation for the Improvement of Living and Working Conditions.

O'Kelly, K.P. and Doyle, P.(1997): 'Workers' Participation in Ireland and the Guinness Brewery Council' in R. Markey and J. Monat (eds.) *Innovation and Employee Participation Through Works Councils*, Aldershot: Avebury.

Olney, S.L. (1996): *Unions in a Changing World: Problems and Prospects in Selected Industrialized Countries,* Geneva: International Labour Office.

O'Mahony, D. (1964): *Industrial Relations in Ireland: The Background,* Dublin: Economic Research Institute.

Osterman, P. (1994): 'How Common Is Workplace Transformation and Who Adopts It?' *Industrial Relations,* Vol. 47, No. 2, 173-88.

Parker, M. and Slaughter, J. (1997): 'Advancing Unionism on the New Terrain' in B. Nissen (ed.): *Unions and Workplace Reorganization,* Michigan: Wayne State University Press.

Peetz, D. (1966): 'Unions, Conflict and the Dilemma of Co-operation', *Journal of Industrial Relations,* Vol. 38. No. 4: 548-570.

Pendleton, A. (1997): 'Characteristics of Workplaces with Financial Participation: Evidence from the Workplace Industrial Relations Survey', *Industrial Relations Journal,* Vol. 28. No. 2: 103-19.

Perline, M.M. (1999): 'Union Views of Managerial Prerogative Revisited: The Prospects for Labour-Management Cooperation', *Journal of Labour Research,* Vol. 20, No. 1: 147-154.

Peterson, R.B. and Lane, T. (1992): 'Assessing Effectiveness of Joint Committees in a Labor-Management Co-operation Program', *Human Relations*, Vol. 45, No. 5, pp 467-88.

Pil, F.K. and McDuffie, J.P. (1996): 'The Adoption of High-Involvement Work Practices', *Industrial Relations*, Vol.35, No. 3, 423- 55.

Rankin, T. and Mansell, J. (1986): 'Integrating Collective Bargaining and New Forms of Work Organization', *National Productivity Review*, Autumn, 1986: 338-47.

Regini, M. (1995): *Uncertain Boundaries: The Social and Political Construction of European Economies*, Cambridge: Cambridge University Press.

Roche, W.K. (1996): *The New Competitive Order and the Fragmentation of Employee Relations in Ireland*, Working Paper, Dublin: Centre for Employment Relations and Organizational Performance, Graduate School of Business, University College Dublin, Blackrock, Co Dublin.

Roche, W.K. (1998): 'Public Service Reform and Human Resource Management', *Administration*, Vol. 46, No. 2.

Roche, W.K. (2002): 'Whither Partnership in the Public Sector?' *Administration*, Vol. 50, No. 4.

Roche, W.K. (2006(a)): 'Critical Issues in Irish Industrial Relations: An Overview of a Changing Landscape', Presentation to Industrial Relations News Conference, Dublin, 9 March 2006.

Roche, W.K. (2006(b)): 'Social Partnership and Workplace Regimes in Ireland', Presentation to Annual Conference of the British Universities' Industrial Relations Association, Galway, June 2006.

Roche, W.K. (2009): 'Who Gains from Partnership?' *The International Journal of Human Resource Management*, Vol. 20, No.1: 1-33.

Roche, W.K. and Geary, J. (2002): 'Advocates, Critics and Union Involvement in Workplace Partnership: Irish Airports', *British Journal of Industrial Relations*, Vol. 40, No. 4: 659-688.

Roche, W.K. and Geary, J.F. (2006): *Partnership at Work: The Quest for Radical Organizational Change*, London: Routledge.

Roche, W.K. and Gunnigle, P (1995): 'Competition and the New Industrial Relations Agenda' in P. Gunnigle and W.K. Roche (eds.) *New Challenges to Irish Industrial Relation*, Dublin: Oak Tree Press.

Roche, W.K. and Kochan, T.A. (1996): *Strategies for Extending Social Partnership to Enterprise and Workplace Levels in Ireland,* unpublished draft paper, Dublin: National Economic and Social Council.

Roche, W.K. and Turner, T. (1998): 'Substitution, Dualism and Partnership: Human Resource Management and Industrial Relations', in W.K Roche, K. Monks and J. Walsh (eds.), *Human Resource Management in Ireland,* Dublin: Oak Tree Press.

Roche, W.K., Geary, J., Brannick, T., Ashmore, J., and Fahy, M. (1998): *Partnership and Involvement in Irish Workplaces,* Report presented to the National Centre for Partnership, Dublin: Centre for Employment Relations and Organizational Performance, Graduate School of Business, University College Dublin.

Rogers, J., and Streeck, W. (1995) (eds.): *Works Councils: Consultation, Representation, and Cooperation in Industrial Relations,* Chicago: University of Chicago Press.

Rosenberg, R.D. and Rosenstein, E. (1980): 'Participation and Productivity: An Empirical Study', *Industrial and Labour Relations Review,* Vol. 33, No. 3, 355-67.

Rubin, B.M. and Rubin, R.S. (2000): 'A Heuristic Model of Collaboration within Labour-Management Relations: Part 2, the Indianapolis Experience', *Journal of Collective Negotiations in the Public Sector,* Vol. 29, No. 2: 139-151.

Rubinstein, S.A. (2000): 'The Impact of Co-management on Quality Performance: the Case of the Saturn Corporation', *Industrial and Labour Relations Review,* Vol. 53, No. 2: 197-218.

Rubinstein, S.A. and Kochan, T.A. (2001): *Learning from Saturn,* Ithaca: ILR Press.

Sabel, C. (1993): 'Studied Trust: Building New Forms of Co-operation in a Volatile Economy', *Human Relations,* Vol. 46, No. 9.

Salamon, M. (2000): *Industrial Relations: Theory and Practice,* Essex: Financial Times/Prentice Hall.

Schein, E.H. (1999): *Process Consultation Revisited: Building the Helping Relationship,* Reading, MA: Addison-Wesley.

Schuster, M. (1983): 'The Impact of Union-Management Co-operation on Productivity and Employment', *Industrial and Labour Relations Review,* Vol. 36, No. 3, 415-30.

Strauss, G. (1998a): 'An Overview', in F. Heller, E. Pusic, G. Strauss, and B. Wilpert (eds.), *Organizational Participation: Myth and Reality,* Oxford: Oxford University Press.

Strauss, G. (1998b), 'Participation Works – If Conditions are Appropriate', in F. Heller, E. Pusic, G. Strauss and B. Wilpert (eds.), *Organizational Participation: Myth and Reality,* Oxford: Oxford University Press.

Streeck, W. (1992): *Social Institutions and Economic Performance,* London: Sage.

Tailby, S., Richardson, M., Upchurch, M., Danford, A., and Stewart, P. (2007): 'Partnership with and without Trade Unions in the UK Financial Services: Filling or Fuelling the Representation Gap?' *Industrial Relations Journal,* 38, 3, 210-228.

Taylor, P. and Ramsay, H. (1998): 'Unions, Partnership and HRM: Sleeping with the Enemy?' *International Journal of Employment Studies,* Vol. 6, No. 2: 115-143.

Teague, P. and Hann, D. (2008): 'Problems with Partnership at Work: Lessons from an Irish Case Study', Paper Commissioned on Behalf of the Labour Relations Commission, Dublin.

Thacker, J.W. and Fields, M. (1987): 'Union Involvement in Quality of Work Life Efforts: A Longitudinal Investigation', *Personnel Psychology,* No. 40, 97-111.

Turner, T., and Morley, M. (1995): *Industrial Relations and the New Order: Case Studies in Conflict and Co-operation,* Dublin: Oak Tree Press.

Verma, A. (1989): 'Joint Participation Programs: Self-help or Suicide for Labor?', *Industrial Relations,* Vol. 28, No. 3, 401-10.

Verma, A. and McKersie, R.B. (1987): 'Employee Involvement: The Implications of Non-involvement by Unions', *Industrial and Labour Relations Review,* Vol. 40, No. 4, 556-68.

von Prondzynski, F. (1995): 'Ireland: Between Centralism and the Market' in A. Ferner and R. Hyman (eds.) *Industrial Relations in the New Europe,* Oxford: Blackwell.

Voos, P. (1987): 'Managerial Perceptions of the Economic Impact of Labour Relations Programmes', *Industrial and Labour Relations Review,* Vol. 40, No. 2, 195-08.

Wallace, J., Gunnigle, P., and McMahon, G. (2004): *Industrial Relations In Ireland*, Dublin: Gill and Macmillan.

Walton, R.E. and McKersie, R.B. (1965): *A Behavioural Theory of Labour Negotiations*, New York: McGraw Hill.

Walton, R.E, Cutcher-Gershenfeld, J.E. and McKersie, R.B. (1994): *Strategic Negotiations: A Theory of Change in Labour-Management Negotiations*, Boston, MA: Harvard Business School Press.

Wells, D. (1991): *What Kind of Unionism is Consistent with the New Model of Human Resource Management?* Working Paper Series, School of Industrial Relations/Industrial Relations Centre, Queen's University at Kingston.

Wells, D. (1993): 'Are Strong Unions Compatible with the New Model of Human Resource Management?', *Relations Industrielles/Industrial Relations*, Vol. 48, No. 1.

Woodworth, W.P. and Meek, C.B. (1994): *Creating Labour–Management Partnerships*, Reading, MA: Addison-Wesley.

INDEX